Initial Public Offerings

Initial Public Offerings

*The mechanics and performance
of IPOs*

Second Edition

Arif Khurshed

Hh

Hh Harriman House

HARRIMAN HOUSE LTD
18 College Street
Petersfield
Hampshire
GU31 4AD
GREAT BRITAIN

Tel: +44 (0)1730 233870
Email: enquiries@harriman-house.com
Website: www.harriman-house.com

First published in Great Britain in 2011
This second edition published in 2019

Copyright © Harriman House Ltd

The right of Arif Khurshed to be identified as Author has been asserted in accordance
with the Copyright, Design and Patents Act 1988.

Paperback ISBN: 978-0-85719-688-0
eBook ISBN: 978-0-85719-689-7

British Library Cataloguing in Publication Data
A CIP catalogue record for this book can be obtained from the British Library.

Contents

About the Author

Arif Khurshed completed his PhD from ICMA Centre, University of Reading, and joined Alliance Manchester Business School (AMBS), University of Manchester, as a post-doctoral researcher. He is a professor of finance in the Division of Accounting & Finance, AMBS.

Arif has taught corporate finance for more than two decades and has been an active researcher in the field of initial public offerings (IPOs), institutional investments, venture capital and corporate governance. He has published his research in several finance journals and has contributed many book chapters. He is currently on the editorial board of the British Accounting Review. Arif has been an external consultant to the UK stock market regulator, the Financial Conduct Authority (formerly FSA) and to the British Venture Capital Association. Now in its second edition, *Initial Public Offerings* was his first book.

Every owner of a physical copy of this edition of

Initial Public Offerings

can download the eBook for free direct from us at Harriman House, in a format that can be read on any eReader, tablet or smartphone.

Simply head to:

ebooks.harriman-house.com/ipos2

to get your free eBook now.

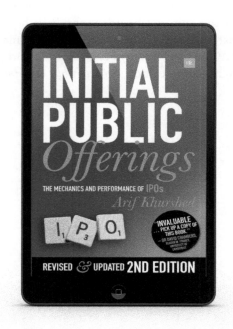

Acknowledgements

I would like to thank Liz Hardy of the London Stock Exchange (LSE) for allowing me to cite and reproduce some material from a survey conducted by the LSE. Thank you to Jay Ritter and Silvio Vismara for their comments and input on an earlier edition of the text. I also thank my family for their patience and support especially during periods of writer's block. I dedicate this book to my wife and two children.

Preface

Since the first edition of this book was published in 2011, much has changed in the world of initial public offerings. The subdued IPO activity during the financial crisis of 2007–09 picked up after 2011. We saw household names such as Facebook and Alibaba (at least in China) conducting successful and record-breaking IPOs. We now await the IPO of the world's largest oil company – Saudi Aramco. If this IPO happens, it is expected to be the biggest the world has ever seen or even imagined at $100bn, giving the company a valuation between $1trn and $2trn.

Companies have also been trying out new methods of conducting an IPO. In April 2018, Swedish music streaming company Spotify conducted a direct listing on the New York Stock Exchange. A direct listing is quite an unconventional way of conducting an IPO; it bypasses most of the arrangements IPO firms make while preparing for their listing. Spotify was successful in its endeavour but it remains to be seen if others will follow. No matter what the outcome of Saudi Aramco listing plans will be, or if direct listings will become fashionable, IPOs will continue to capture our imagination.

In this second edition of the book, I have updated most of the chapters to include information on the developments in the IPO world since 2011. The short case studies in Chapter 2 now include analysis of Facebook's, Alibaba's and Royal Mail's IPOs. All of these were unique in some way. Over the last few years, research on IPOs has shed new light on their performance and survival, and on the role of grey markets and trading around lockup expiry. The format of the IPO prospectus has also changed. A discussion of these developments is now embedded in the appropriate chapters.

What this book covers

This book is about one of the most attractive areas of investment, Initial Public Offerings (IPOs), commonly referred to as new issues. Reducing an IPO to its very basics, it refers to the occasion when a company issues common stock or shares to the public for the first time. The IPO process is also known as going public, flotation and listing, and throughout this book I use these terms interchangeably.

IPOs have considerable appeal since they allow investors to buy shares in exciting new companies as they make their debut on the stock exchange. In addition, there is the lure of making potentially high returns in a relatively short period of time, as quite often on the first day of trading the share price of these companies closes much higher than the price at which the shares were offered to investors in the IPO.

The main purpose of the book is to provide information on the mechanics and performance of IPOs. Readers will find information on some fundamental questions related to investment in IPO markets, including the different methods of flotation, how IPOs are priced, and the performance of IPOs in the short and long term. The book also provides some information related to investing in the IPO market, including where to find information and how an IPO prospectus is structured.

Who this book is for

This book is for investors, academics and students who want to find out more about how IPOs are arranged and their historic performance. Entrepreneurs and directors of companies planning an IPO will also find this book helpful.

How this book is structured

This book is organised into the following chapters:

- **An Introduction to IPOs**: This chapter covers some basic information on going public such as the life cycle of companies, and why and when companies go public. It also discusses how companies prepare for an IPO.

- **A History of IPOs**: This chapter begins with a discussion of the regulatory and administrative history of UK IPOs at the London Stock Exchange (LSE). A discussion of share trading on LSE follows. The third section of the chapter provides a brief history of IPOs in the UK since 1945. In the last part of the chapter I discuss some high-profile UK and international IPOs.

- **Mechanics of IPOs**: This chapter looks at the dynamics of an IPO, such as the different methods by which a firm can do an IPO on the LSE and their implications for potential investors. Information is included on how IPOs are priced, how to apply for shares and how share allocations are made in practice. There is also a look at when shares are received by investors and when can they be traded.

- **The Performance and Survival of IPOs**: This chapter looks at what happens once a company successfully lists on the stock market. When investors buy shares in an IPO firm, they expect healthy profits from their investment. Are their profits really healthy? What happens if the investors decide not to sell their shares in the immediate aftermarket but to hold on to their investments for a longer period of time? Will the IPO firm survive long enough to provide a good return on investment? Questions like these are answered in this chapter using historic and current data on LSE IPOs.

- **Investing in IPOs**: This chapter looks at where to find information on firms planning an IPO, what the IPO prospectus says about the quality of the firm, and what factors identify good or bad IPO investments.

1

An Introduction to IPOs

In this chapter I start with a discussion of the life cycle of companies and how some of them move towards an IPO. The next section discusses why companies may decide to conduct an IPO, and the potential disadvantages of such a decision. A discussion of how companies prepare for an IPO follows.

1.1 The life cycle of companies

Businesses in the private sector are started either as unincorporated or incorporated concerns. Unincorporated businesses fall into two types depending on whether there is a single owner (sole trader) or several owners (partnership). With an unincorporated business there is no legal distinction between the business and its owner(s).

Incorporated businesses have a separate legal identity from their owners. Of these, the commonest form are companies limited by shares. They can be private or public limited companies. Private limited companies can only sell their shares or debentures privately but public limited companies (PLCs) can raise capital from the public at large through an IPO.

Both unincorporated and incorporated businesses are initially funded by the founder owners and as these firms grow they need more capital. The owners may first turn to their friends and family when they need additional funds. Later they may borrow from a bank either as a fixed-term loan or through an overdraft facility. When such sources are exhausted, firms may turn towards private equity providers such as business angels and venture capitalists (VCs).

1

For those firms which do not have such an option (VCs have preferences for certain types of firms in certain industry sectors), an alternative is to list the company on a stock exchange through an IPO. Even for VC-backed firms, there may come a time when the VC would like to exit the firm in order to capitalise on its investment. On the occasion of such an exit of the VC from a firm, one of two usual methods is used – trade sales or, again, an IPO.

For any firm to conduct an IPO, it has to be a public limited company (PLC). So if a firm was started as a sole trading firm, it would need to incorporate itself as a PLC before it would be allowed to go public. Figure 1.1 provides an illustration of the situation as described so far for UK private enterprise.

Figure 1.1 – UK businesses in the private sector

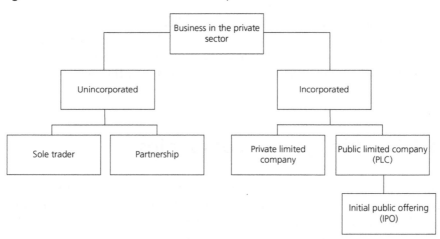

Not all companies choose the path of an IPO. In fact, in any country only a small fraction of firms end up doing an IPO. For example, in the UK, of the 2.67m firms registered for VAT and/or PAYE in March 2018, only around 2,200 or so are listed on the London Stock Exchange (LSE).

1.2 Why companies conduct IPOs

Companies conduct an IPO for a variety of reasons. For instance, growing companies need capital for expansion. If internal sources such as retained earnings and friends and family, or external sources such as bank loans or private equity, are either unavailable or do not generate sufficient capital then usually the only option left for a firm that needs funding is to conduct an IPO.

An IPO helps the company in more than one way. Through an IPO a firm can raise capital to finance its current and future capital requirements. A part of this capital can be used to retire debt by paying off overdrafts or loans which are close to maturity. Also, once an IPO has been completed, companies can further raise capital in the future by conducting seasoned equity offerings (called rights issues in the UK). Thirdly, companies that have conducted an IPO can expect to borrow on better terms in the market because of the better transparency surrounding the company's business and accounts that comes from its listing on the stock exchange.

Another reason why firms may wish to go public is for employee compensation. A large number of firms believe that by offering employees a formal stake (shares with a market price) in the company, they are offering an incentive to work hard. Share ownership may also help the firm to retain high quality staff. When Moneysupermarket conducted an IPO in July 2007, it offered free shares to its employees. In an interview a spokeswoman for Moneysupermarket said:

> Indeed, one of the core reasons for the flotation is to be able to offer the employee share schemes in respect of listed securities. This will not only allow staff to enjoy the success of the business, but will help to attract and retain employees.[1]

The chief executive of Moneysupermarket went on to add:

> Every single member of staff is getting free shares worth a minimum of £3,000. Even a receptionist who has been in the business for two months.[2]

A similar theme was attached to the Admiral Group IPO in 2004 in which the employees had an 8% stake. Alastair Lyons, chairman of Admiral, said:

> Flotation is a key stage in the group's development, enabling us to provide a public market for Admiral shares, increasing the profile of the group and enabling employees to see the benefit of their work.[3]

In a recent report, professional services firm Deloitte found that over a quarter of companies doing an IPO in the UK gave free shares to all employees. A partner in the remuneration team at Deloitte commented:

---

1   www.personneltoday.com
2   *Daily Telegraph.*
3   *Post Magazine*, 15 September 2004.

Companies listing today are increasingly using the IPO as an opportunity to give shares to all their employees and are not just focussed on senior management. An IPO requires commitment from all employees but provides the opportunity to introduce share plans which motivate the employees during this process. These plans can not only be used to help lock-in key executives and senior management but are also a great way to reward all employees and to share in the value created from a successful IPO.[4]

There are strategic advantages that occur once an IPO has been completed. When a firm goes public, its reputation and visibility are enhanced, thus giving it a vital competitive edge over its unlisted competitors. When a firm is private, its operations are usually constrained by limited capital as potential acquirers simply do not know of the firm's existence. A public listing makes it easier for companies to notice and evaluate the firm for potential mergers or acquisitions.

Going public also has benefits for a company's founder owners. A public listing provides a good opportunity for the entrepreneur to sell some of his or her stake in the company so as to consume some of the capital tied up in the business. An IPO is also a chance for the proprietor to reduce the risk of their investment portfolio by diversifying into a wider spread of investments.

Various benefits of going public are perhaps best illustrated using the example of womenswear retailer Quiz Plc which did an IPO on the LSE in July 2017. In its listing prospectus, the company provided details of the reasons for its going public and the use of IPO proceeds:

> The board believes that admission will be an important step in the group's development and will assist in achieving its growth and profitability ambitions.

> The board intends to use the gross proceeds from the placing of new shares of £10.6m receivable by the company as follows:

> • approximately £6m on marketing and advertising, and in particular to support the company's expansion into mainland Europe and the US;

> • approximately £2.0m to fund further capital expenditure and operating costs required to support the company's continued growth, and in particular, IT infrastructure; and

> • approximately £2.6m on admission expenses, additional working capital and broadening Quiz's product range.

---

4   Deloitte press release, 3 April 2014.

In addition, board expects that the placing and admission will provide a public market for the ordinary shares, which will benefit employee shareholders, and will enable the company, if required, to access the capital markets for additional finance to support its strategic objectives.

The net proceeds of £89.8m from the placing of sale shares receivable by the selling shareholders will enable the selling shareholders who founded Quiz to realise, in part, their investment in the company.[5]

Not all reasons why businesses conduct IPOs are of equal importance. In a survey of firms that listed during the early 2000s, LSE found that for 71% of the firms that listed on LSE, the main reason for listing was the need to raise funds for growth. It was found that 11% of the surveyed firms mentioned enhancement of the company's profile and credibility as the main reason for their listing. A similar percentage mentioned exit of VC investors as the main reason for seeking a stock market flotation. Only 5% of the firms felt that the main reason for an IPO was to provide share options to directors and staff. Another 5% mentioned future acquisitions as the key motive.

When looking at an IPO, it is important to check what the raised funds will be used for – at different times it might be best for companies to use capital in certain ways. For example, at times when the wider economy is contracting (as during the credit crunch and falling stock markets of 2007–09), investors may not wish to invest in an IPO firm that has no good plans for growth and instead intends to use most of the cash raised from the IPO to pay its debt.

IPO companies that are a management buyout (MBO), or firms which have had VC backing, usually borrow money to pay a dividend to pre-IPO shareholders such as the VCs, buyout firms and banks. This borrowed money is then repaid using the proceeds of the IPO. An example of such a case is Verso Paper, which did an IPO on NYSE in May 2008. Verso mentioned in its listing prospectus that almost 99% of the proceeds of the IPO would be used to pay the debt incurred in making payments to its equity holders.

Similarly, RHI Entertainment, which went public on NASDAQ in June 2008, also used the funds raised to repay debt. Verso Paper and RHI Entertainment have both been poor performers when compared with other IPOs. On the first day of trading, shares of Verso Paper closed nearly 17% below their offer price. In early January 2011, Verso's shares were trading nearly 70% below the offer price. Eventually its share price recovered; by early 2018, Verso was trading above the offer price of $12. RHI had problems in finding buyers for its IPO shares and its offer price was set below the expected range.

---

5   Excerpt from Quiz Plc's admission document (pages 35 and 36).

If a firm says that it is planning to use most of its proceeds from an IPO to retire debt then close attention should be paid to the company's financial data, its business plan (once the issue proceeds have been used to pay off the debt) and the overall growth prospects for the firm's industry. There is more discussion on this in Chapter 5.

A note on primary and secondary shares

In an IPO a business will typically sell two types of shares: primary and secondary. Technically there is no difference between these two types of shares. The difference only lies in their source.

Though the financial requirements of the business are a strong motivation for going public, the sale of existing shares (secondary shares, owned by the owners of the business) does not affect the business financially – the proceeds from the sale of secondary shares go only to the owners of the shares. It is only the sale of newly created shares (primary shares) that bring money to the firm's accounts at the time of the IPO. As stated, most IPOs offer a mix of both primary and secondary shares.

It is important to note that this combination of primary and secondary shares differs from market to market. Jenkinson and Ljungqvist report that 67% of Portuguese IPOs involve shares sold by insiders in the business only, while for Germany the proportion is 23%.[6] This means that in nearly seven out of ten IPOs in Portugal (and two out of ten in Germany) the IPO is only done in order for the entrepreneur to exit (or partially exit) from the firm. In these cases no money is raised on behalf of the firm as all the shares that are sold are secondary.

By contrast, 98% of US IPOs involve at least some primary equity while 56% sell only primary equities. The average split between primary and secondary equity of the US is 85% and 15% respectively. For the UK market, Brennan and Franks report the split between primary and secondary equity to be around 54% and 46%.[7] In Finland 73% of equity sold in IPOs is primary.

The mix of primary and secondary shares being sold by a firm in an IPO is usually mentioned in the listing prospectus and can be revealing. For example, if all the shares on sale only come from the existing owners – they are all secondary shares – this would be alarming as it would signal a *cash in and run* from the owners.

---

[6] T. J. Jenkinson and A. P. Ljungqvist, *Going Public: The Theory and Evidence on How Companies Raise Equity Finance* (Oxford University Press, 2001).

[7] M.J. Brennan and J. Franks, 'Underpricing, ownership and control in initial public offerings of equity securities in the UK', *Journal of Financial Economics* 45 (1997), pp. 391–413.

Disadvantages of IPOs

There are disadvantages to going public, as well as benefits. When firms do an IPO, they have to adhere to strict transparency rules covering information about the company. Various aspects of the management, such as the board structure, directors' remuneration and insider dealings come under public scrutiny. Further, the listed company has to adhere to continuing obligations once it is listed in that it has to disclose price sensitive information and has to regularly file reports with the financial regulators and the stock exchange.

All this costs money and time, and it also provides vital strategic information to the firm's competitors. In the LSE survey of the early 2000s mentioned above, nearly all the surveyed companies identified certain drawbacks to being listed on the stock exchange. Primary amongst these drawbacks (with 61% of companies citing it) was the need for additional reporting and its associated costs. In addition, nearly 34% of firms were concerned about the volatility of their share price.

Thinking more broadly about the downsides of an IPO, one of the main outcomes is that the management becomes separate from ownership. The owners of the firm appoint the board of directors who in turn appoint managers who run the firm on a day-to-day basis. This may lead to managerial short-sightedness in that the managers systematically reject good investment opportunities with long time horizons. Going public may also bring out problems associated with the classic principal-agent conflict, in that not all the decisions taken by the management are in the interests of the owners of the firm.

A further consideration is that while going public increases the visibility of a firm meaning mergers are more likely, it does also open up the possibility of a hostile takeover where the owners of the firm may lose control of their business.

Finally, conducting an IPO is not cheap. As Table 1.1 shows, for firms conducting small IPOs at the LSE the total costs could be around 11% of the total funds raised. In other words, for every £1 raised in the IPO the firm pays out around 11p as a cost. However, there are economies of scale as the size of the funds raised increases. Large IPOs – those that raise £35m and above, for example – pay around 4% as the cost of the IPO. As discussed, an IPO is a time-consuming process, so other indirect costs such as management's time and effort cannot be ignored.

Table 1.1 – Costs of conducting an IPO

Funds raised from flotation (£'000)	Total costs as % of funds raised
1,000–5,000	11
5,001–8,500	8
8,501–16,500	5
16,501–35,000	4
35,001 and above	4

Source: Adapted from M. Goergen, A. Khurshed and R. Mudambi, 'The Strategy of Going Public: How UK firms choose their listing contracts', *Journal of Business Finance & Accounting*, vol. 33(1-2), pp. 79–101 (2006).

Alternative ways of listing on a stock market

Apart from an IPO, there are other ways in which a firm can obtain a listing on a stock exchange. One such method is a reverse takeover. In a reverse takeover, a firm wishing to list on a stock exchange (private firm) merges with a firm already listed on the exchange (publicly-traded firm, sometimes also known as a shell firm). The owners of the private firm control the combined publicly-traded firm. After the reverse takeover is complete, the combined firm usually changes its name and reinvents itself. Though listing through a reverse takeover is quite cheap and can take place relatively faster than an IPO, this method of listing hasn't been as popular as the proponents would have wished.

Spotify, the Swedish music, podcast and video streaming service listed on the New York Stock Exchange (NYSE) in early April 2018 using a 'direct listing'. In a direct listing, shares are offered to new investors directly without the help of intermediaries (such as the sponsor or the underwriter). No new shares are issued and only existing shares are made available to new investors. This method is cheap, democratic and more decentralised than a traditional IPO. However, there are certain risks involved in using a direct listing. There is no support or guarantee that the listing will be successful. There are no road shows, no price support in the aftermarket and it's the market that ultimately sets the price. In the case of Spotify, the NYSE set Spotify's reference price at $132 per share. The reference price is not the offering price or the opening price on the first day of trading. The opening price is set by matching the buy and sell orders from broker-dealers on the first day of trading. For Spotify, the opening price was

$165.90. However by the end of the first trading day, the price had fallen to $149. It stayed around this level over the first two weeks of listing.

Both reverse takeovers and direct listings are an alternative to an IPO but remain low-key methods which may be suitable for some companies but not all.

1.3 Company preparation for an IPO

Satisfying requirements

Companies that plan to conduct an IPO on the Main Market of the LSE can choose between a Premium Listing and a Standard Listing. A Premium Listing requires that a company meets standards that are over and above those set forth in EU legislation, as well as the UK's Corporate Governance Code. For a Standard Listing, the company has to meet the requirements laid down by the EU legislation with a lighter compliance burden. Companies conducting an IPO have to abide by two sets of rules: those of the UK Listing Authority (UKLA), which is a division of the Financial Conduct Authority (FCA) and the LSE's Admission and Disclosure Requirements. The UKLA has the responsibility for the approval of prospectuses and admission of companies to the Main Market. The LSE is responsible for the admission to trading of companies to the Main Market. This situation is shown in Figure 1.2.

Figure 1.2 – Joining the Main Market of LSE

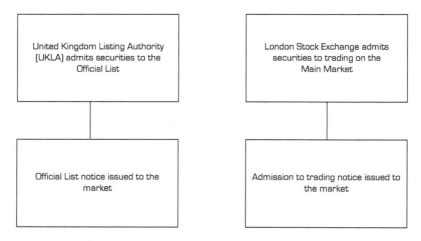

Source: Adapted from 'A Guide to Listing on the London Stock Exchange' 2017.

When applying to UKLA for permission to conduct an IPO, a firm has to satisfy certain principal requirements, including:[8]

- *Incorporation*: The company must be incorporated. This means that UK companies should be a PLC at the time of application.

- *Accounts*: The company must publish audited accounts that cover a three-year period. The period for which the audited accounts are submitted and the planned flotation should not be more than six months apart.

- *Track record*: The company must have carried on as an independent business in the three-year period covered by the audited accounts submitted. Also, if the company has made a large number of acquisitions in the three years up to listing then it must show that these firms have a suitable track record as well.

- *Directors*: The company's directors must demonstrate a collective experience and expertise to run the business and must be free of conflicts of interest.

- *Working capital*: The company must be able to demonstrate that it has a sufficient working capital to meet current and projected requirements (taking into account the flotation proceeds) for at least the next 12 months. This requirement is only for companies seeking a Premium Listing.

---

[8]   These requirements have been adapted from, 'Listing Rules', Financial Conduct Authority Handbook 2018.

- *Independent operations*: The company must be able to carry on its business independently and at arm's length from any shareholders with a 30% or more interest in the company.

- *Shares in public hands*: As a result of listing at least 25% of the shares must be in public hands (public float). The UKLA sometimes allows companies with large market capitalisations to have a free float smaller than 25%.

- *Market capitalisation*: The expected aggregate market value of all securities to be listed must be at least £700,000.

Mineral companies and scientific research companies are subject to additional listing requirements, although they are not required to have a three-year, revenue earning, audited track record.

Players in the IPO process

An IPO is a complex and time-consuming process in which a number of players are involved, the company itself being one of them. Once a company decides that it wants to conduct an IPO, it has to identify and then appoint professional advisors to help the firm prepare for its flotation. The experts and organisations that help a firm to prepare for an IPO are:

1. Sponsor

2. Corporate broker (book runner)

3. Accountant

4. Lawyers

5. Registrars

6. Other advisers, including PR consultants and chartered surveyors

We will now look at these in turn.

1. The sponsor

The FCA listing rules make it mandatory for any firm wishing to list on the Main Market of the London Stock Exchange through a Premium Listing to appoint a sponsor (also known as an underwriter). An investment bank, a stock broker, an accountant or a corporate finance house could be a sponsor provided they are approved by the UKLA to fulfill this role.

The sponsor plays the most important role in the IPO process and advises the firm on almost all aspects of a listing including the appointment of other professional advisers, such as the brokers, accountants, lawyers and a PR agency (if needed).

Choosing the right sponsor is one of the first things a firm has to do and it is a difficult task. Usually existing advisers would be consulted on who should be appointed as the IPO sponsor. The firm shortlists a few potential sponsors based on their expertise, experience, reputation and likely fees, and invites them to attend an assessment called a beauty parade. As a part of the beauty parade, the firm usually queries the potential sponsors about their estimates on the valuation of the firm (i.e. the price at which the firm will offer its shares to the market) and about the likely interest from different types of investors (retail and institutional) in the firm's offering.

Sometimes the company may select a sponsor for reasons other than those already mentioned, as was evident in the case of the eBay IPO, where eBay appointed Goldman Sachs as its underwriter. It later emerged that eBay officers (CEO, chairman and vice president) received shares of other IPO companies from Goldman Sachs over a long period of time (a practice known as spinning), which they were able to sell at substantial profits. In return for this the eBay management hired Goldman Sachs as the underwriter to the firm's IPO. eBay shareholders subsequently sued the executives, arguing that they should have used the share allocations to benefit the company, rather than for personal gain.[9] The eBay executives settled their shareholder lawsuit by paying $3.395m to eBay. Goldman Sachs also paid $395,000. IPO lawsuits are quite common in the US but are rare in the UK.

The appointment of a sponsor is not totally in the hands of the IPO firm, as sponsors themselves can be picky when it comes to bringing a company for an IPO. In the investment banking industry, reputation is priceless. Highly reputed sponsors would not wish to be associated with a firm which is of a bad quality or which is bringing a small IPO to the market and so they might not agree to work with a firm which they believe falls into this category.

Once a sponsor has been appointed, it is the sponsor's job to make a diligent assessment of the company's suitability for an IPO. It will advise the company on the structure and make-up of the board of directors and any restructuring of the capital, if needed. For example, on the advice of its sponsors, EasyJet spent almost a year before its IPO hiring a distinguished group of non-executive directors to enhance the transparency of its board. The sponsor will also advise the firm on the best method of flotation, the flotation timetable and the pricing and underwriting of the shares.

---

9   Xiaoding Liu and Jay Ritter of University of Florida have studied the economic consequences of IPO spinning. They found that IPOs in which executives are being *spun* are more underpriced and companies whose directors are being spun are less likely to switch underwriters for their first seasoned equity offering. Liu and Ritter (2010).

The sponsor in an AIM listing

For those firms that wish to list on the junior segment of the London Stock Exchange, AIM, rather than the Main Market, a sponsor per se is not required. Instead, a professional adviser (the Nominated Adviser or Nomad) helps the firms with its IPO.

The role of the Nomad is similar to that of a sponsor until the time the firm lists on the stock exchange, but a difference emerges in the post-IPO period. After the listing, sponsors have a limited role (such as price stabilisation, if required) but Nomads will continue to be associated with the firms when they are listed on AIM. This is a regulatory requirement from the LSE. If at any point of time (in the post-IPO period) the firm loses its Nomad, its shares will be temporarily suspended from trading till the time a new Nomad is appointed by the firm.

2. Corporate broker (book runner)

A broker connects an IPO firm to the stock market and to potential investors. It will assess the conditions on the stock market at the time the IPO is being planned and the likely interest of investors for the company's shares. It will also actively market the IPO shares to potential investors. A broker is sometimes called a book runner because it is responsible for running the order book of demand which is built during the book building period.

If required, the broker can provide advice on the method of listing (placing or offer for sale, which we will examine in more detail later); the size of the offering; the timing of the IPO; and the offer price. It can also arrange underwriting and placing agreements and helps the firm to meet its listing requirements. The role of the broker does not end when the IPO is successfully conducted. It continues to work with the firm in the post-flotation period to maintain shares' liquidity and the company's profile in the aftermarket.

Sometimes both the sponsorship and stock broking/book building services can be provided by the same firm. The IPO firm can choose whether it wishes to appoint a single firm providing both these services – usually economies of scale make it a cheaper option. The same is also true with listing on the AIM; a Nomad can act as an adviser and also as a stock broker for the firm.

3. Accountant

The accountants have a key role to play in the IPO process. They review the company's financial record and produce a detailed report on the company's financial controls and the projected working capital requirements for at least a year after the IPO. This report is called the *long form report* and is primarily produced to help the firm and the sponsors to draft the listing prospectus.

The long form report forms the basis of the *short form report* that is included in the listing prospectus. Apart from this important function, the reporting accountants also advise the firm on the tax implications of the IPO. Some firms may wish to appoint separate tax specialists for this purpose.

The reporting accountant in an IPO has to be different from the existing company auditors. However, it could be a separate team in the same firm. An IPO firm may wish to appoint the reporting accountant from a totally different firm in order to avoid any conflicts of interest and to ensure the highest level of detachment and independence.

4. Lawyers

According to the LSE, most IPO firms have two separate sets of lawyers; one that advises the company and its existing shareholders and the other that acts as a solicitor to the sponsor. The company lawyers focus on legal issues such as changes to company's articles of association, directors' contracts and, if need be, re-registering the company as a PLC. If the company requires, they may also draft the share option plans for the company's employees.

As every single statement made in the listing prospectus has to be verified as true, the company lawyers are responsible for preparing the verification questions to confirm the facts. These lawyers work alongside the sponsor's lawyers when it comes to any agreements between the company, its existing shareholders and the sponsor. Usually these agreements relate to such things as underwriting and tax issues.

5. Registrars

The listing company has to appoint company registrars, whose job is to keep records of the share ownership. They hold the company's register and issue share certificates.

6. Other advisers that may be required

Besides these main players there are some other advisers a company may wish to appoint for the IPO process. For example, some companies may wish to appoint a PR consultant in order to create awareness in the market. Amongst other things, PR consultants ensure that any public statements or press releases by the firm are permissible under the relevant disclosure regulations. They also help to generate some positive press. Green Rubber Global, a UK based tyre recycling firm which planned an IPO on AIM in November 2008, brought in none other than Hollywood actor Mel Gibson to promote its IPO.[10]

---

10 The company could not float on AIM because of difficult market conditions in

Occasionally, the firm considering an IPO may wish to appoint chartered surveyors or valuers to assess property values; specialist printers for the production of prospectuses and other related documents; actuaries to assess the company pension schemes; receivers to handle share applications; and insurance companies to check if all risks are adequately covered.

Lastly, the stock exchange itself is fundamental to the success of the IPO and beyond. The stock exchange has a legal obligation to oversee the listing process. It mostly deals with the company sponsor or broker but sometimes when needed it gets in touch with the company. The ongoing role of the stock exchange is to ensure that the company makes the best use of its listing and that it receives the maximum benefit from its listing.

2008. Its parent company, Petra Group was later sued by another Hollywood actor Bruce Willis for withholding $900,000 of the $2m investment the actor had made in the business.

2

A History of IPOs

In this chapter I look at the regulatory and administrative history of UK IPOs. This includes a focus on share trading on the London Stock Exchange (LSE) and a discussion of some important UK and international IPOs that have come to the market in the last few years. The chapter also includes a brief history of IPOs in the UK since 1945.

2.1 The London Stock Exchange

The LSE is one of the oldest stock exchanges in the world and one can trace its history back to 17th century coffee houses, which is where organised trading of marketable securities first took place. However, it was not until 1801 that the modern stock exchange was born.

Today, LSE is the largest stock exchange in Europe and the third largest in the world in terms of market capitalisation of listed firms.[11] By the end of 2018, there were nearly 2,100 companies with a total market value of over £3,876bn listed on the LSE. The exchange attracts all types of companies, including small, large, start-ups, domestic and global firms. It is also the most international stock exchange in the world.

The biggest change that LSE has been through in recent memory was its deregulation on 27 October 1986. This deregulation of the LSE is known as Big Bang (BB). Amongst other changes, the most noticeable were an end to

---

[11] NYSE Euronext is the largest whereas NASDAQ is the second largest.

face-to-face trading on the stock exchange floor, and the exchange becoming a private limited company under the Companies Act 1985.

Before BB, nearly all trades took place on the trading floor of the Stock Exchange but henceforward trading on the floor ceased. The new trading system relied on a computerised price display called SEAQ (Stock Exchange Automated Quotation system). With SEAQ, traders could see buying and selling prices on computer screens and finalise deals by telephone. The pre and post-BB trading systems were both quote-driven. Jobbers, and subsequently market makers, quoted bid-ask prices verbally and subsequently on computer screens.

In October 1997 an order-driven system was introduced for the FTSE 100 shares, operated entirely electronically. This is called SETS (Stock Exchange Electronic Trading Service). Under SETS, computer screens display customers' buying and selling orders. If the orders are *limit orders* the screen will also display the buying and selling price. If the orders are at *best* the transaction takes place at the highest available buying price (for a sell order) or the lowest available selling price (for a buy order).

Other types of orders are *fill or kill* orders, which are executed immediately if they can be satisfied in full from an order already on the book, and *execute* or *eliminate* orders, which can be executed in part immediately, but with the portion unmatched immediately deleted. The computerised system automatically matches and clears orders; when a buyer's bid price and a seller's offer price match, orders automatically execute against one another on the screen. SETS is currently used for around 1,000 of the most liquid firms on the FTSE All-Share Index, and for exchange traded funds (ETFs), exchange traded commodities (ETCs) and nearly 180 of the most traded Alternative Investment Market (AIM) and Irish securities. SEAQ is used for securities that trade less regularly.

The LSE is organised into two markets:

1. The Main Market (also known as the Official List)

2. The Alternative Investment Market (AIM)

Figure 2.1 provides an illustration of these two markets.

Figure 2.1 – The two markets of the LSE

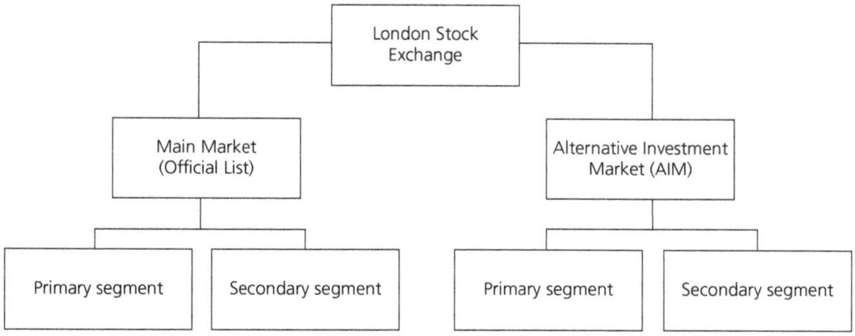

The Main Market

The Main Market of the LSE is commonly identified as the UK stock market. It is the oldest market of the LSE and is regarded as the world's most international market for an IPO and subsequent trading of company shares. As of the end of 2018, there were over 1,160 companies from 44 countries listed on the Main Market.

The Main Market boasts one of the world's most respected sets of listing and disclosure standards. Once a company lists on this market it has to follow the rules and guidelines set by the LSE (referred to as ongoing obligations) in order to maintain transparency towards the shareholders.

Companies considering an IPO on the Main Market are required to meet the eligibility standards set out by the UKLA's Listing Rules (discussed earlier). Some of these criteria are equivalent to the harmonised standards set by EU Directives. However, UK-domiciled firms wishing to list on the Main Market have to satisfy additional requirements, which are termed *super-equivalent* to European standards.

The following requirements have to be complied with:

- LSE's Admission and Disclosure Standards

- Appointment of a sponsor

- Listing Principles

- Listing prospectus approved by the UKLA

- Free transferability of securities

Within the Main Market there are certain sectors in which several companies are grouped together. One of the most well-known is techMARK. It went live on 4 November 1999 with over 190 UK and international companies from a wide range of FTSE industrial sectors across the main market, whose success depends on technological innovation. techMARK is open to innovative technology companies with a primary or dual primary listing in London, irrespective of their size, industrial classification or location. The purpose of techMARK is to create a new way for growing technology companies to access capital to finance expansion. There is also techMARK mediscience, a market for healthcare companies.

The share price performance of companies listed on the Main Market of the LSE is tracked using a variety of indices. A stock index is an indicator which is used to measure the changes in share prices of a group of companies in a particular segment of a stock exchange. The index that covers all the companies listed on the Main Market is the FTSE All-Share Index. The FTSE 100 tracks the performance of the largest 100 firms (in terms of market capitalisation) on the LSE.

The Alternative Investment Market (AIM)

AIM is still a relatively new market, started in 1995, to allow small and fast-growing companies a chance to conduct an IPO.[12] It has light-touch regulations in comparison to the Main Market, making it possible for firms which otherwise would not be allowed to list on the Main Market to conduct an IPO and list on AIM.

One of the ways in which the rules of AIM are less stringent is that there is no requirement for any freefloat for AIM firms. This means there is no regulation on the proportion of company shares that must be available for purchase by investors unrelated to the firm at the time of an IPO. In addition, AIM firms do not have to be of any minimum market capitalisation or have any prior trading record before listing.

One thing that all AIM companies are required to have is a Nominated Adviser (Nomad), responsible for warranting that the company is appropriate for AIM. Indeed, on AIM, neither the LSE nor the UKLA are required to approve the prospectus when the listing is not preceded by a public offer of securities, relying instead on the Nomad to ensure compliance.

---

[12] The AIM replaced the USM (Unlisted Securities Market) that was set up in 1980 to cater for smaller companies, but met only limited success and was closed at the end of 1996. A previous attempt to establish a market for smaller stocks, the Third Market, flopped in the wake of the 1987 stock market crash, and was finally closed in 1990.

This opportunity (created by the Public Offer of Securities 1995 and the Financial Services and Markets Act 2000 regulations) would have vanished with the introduction of the Prospectus Directive in July 2005, which required any issuer admitted to trading on a regulated market to produce an UKLA-approved prospectus. However, to preserve this different regulatory regime for AIM IPOs, the LSE was forced to change the status of the AIM from *regulated* market to *exchange-regulated* market at the end of 2004.

Under the AIM rules, all companies must produce an Admission Document making certain disclosures about matters such as their directors' backgrounds, business activities, financial position and promoters. The content of the Admission Document must satisfy the same criteria as the EU prospectus required by the Prospectus Directive only when listing is preceded by a public offer of securities. In all other situations the Admission Document is required to present a narrower set of information. This particular status gives a high degree of freedom to the AIM and it is considered a fundamental ingredient of AIM's appeal as a successful marketplace for young and growing companies.

Figure 2.2 – Listing activity on AIM

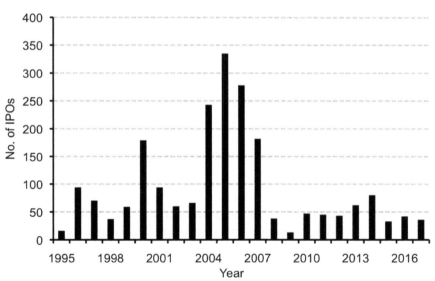

Source: Data from London Stock Exchange 2017.

Since its inception, AIM has continued to grow, even during the aftermath of the dot-com bubble and the sub-prime crisis, when almost all the stock markets in the world saw a fall in the number of IPOs. Today AIM is amongst the most successful second tier markets in the world, with more than 925 listed companies of which around 200 are from abroad. Figure 2.2 shows the IPO activity in AIM since its launch in 1995.

AIM is now seen as a model by the other stock markets in mainland Europe when trying to (re)launch second-tier markets such as Euronext or the Expandi in Italy;[13] or OTCQX in the US. Even though several second and new markets were created in continental Europe during the last two decades, none of them was successful in becoming an effective second-tier market.

Other markets in London

OFEX – later renamed PLUS Market (now defunct)

The Off Exchange (OFEX) was started in 1995 as an unregulated market where unlisted and unquoted securities were traded. In fact, OFEX had been around before 1995 in some form or other. In 2002 OFEX became a prescribed market, authorised and regulated by the FCA. In 2003 OFEX Holdings Plc itself became a quoted company on AIM. A year later, following refinancing and changes in board and management team, OFEX was renamed as PLUS Markets Group Plc. In 2007 PLUS was recognised as a stock exchange by the FCA. PLUS was a market for small firms in need of money for growth. It was sometimes referred to as a third-tier market.

When firms conducted an IPO on PLUS they had to appoint a PLUS Corporate Adviser, who has a similar role to that of a Nomad for AIM firms. This Corporate Adviser acted as the sponsor to the IPO. The need to appoint other players such as accountants, solicitors, etc., was the same as in other markets. The entry criteria were not as stringent as those for the AIM and Main Market companies. At one point of time more than 160 companies were listed on PLUS, including Arsenal Football Club.

PLUS was launched to compete with the LSE's AIM market. However, it got into financial difficulty, and in May 2012 announced that it would close. PLUS Stock Exchange and its derivatives operations were later bought by interdealer broker ICAP.

---

[13] Thomson Ventureconomics (22 June 2004): 'Euronext, the European stock exchange, is launching its own version of the London Stock Exchange's successful Alternative Investment Market' (www.ventureeconomics.com).

2.2 Regulatory and administrative history of UK IPOs

Historically, IPOs on the LSE were conducted under the Rules and Regulations of the Stock Exchange, which were quite different to those in place today. These days when a firm conducts an IPO, it has to publish a document called a prospectus that is designed to provide information to prospective investors. However, early in the 20th century, there is evidence that a large number of firms conducted an IPO on the LSE without issuing a prospectus at all.[14]

In an attempt to force companies to provide more information, the LSE introduced rules in 1919 which made it mandatory for a firm to have an advertised statement in the press (in place of a prospectus) before the exchange allowed the firm to list.[15]

However, such disclosure did not include information on the financial performance and health of the firm.[16] So lax were the LSE rules at this time that they amounted to no more than four pages in total and there were no stipulated minimum listing criteria. These regulations were significantly revised after 1945.

In the early 1950s, rules were introduced that required IPO firms to disclose a ten-year track record in their IPO prospectus (though this was reduced to five years before the 1970s). In addition, under these updated rules, the firms had to be of a minimum market capitalisation of £100,000 and at the time of the IPO were required to sell at least 25% of their shares to investors not related to the firm (this is called *freefloat*).

In 1973 the LSE rules on IPOs came to be known as the Admission of Securities to Listing, or the Yellow Book.[17] By the end of 1970s, this Yellow Book had over 100 pages dealing with listing requirements and the relevant documentation alone. When LSE created a junior partner to its Main Market in 1981, the Unlisted Securities Market (USM), it required USM IPOs to show a track record of only three years and a freefloat of only 10%.

Until Big Bang in 1986, the LSE made its own rules on listing, including the minimum disclosure requirements at the time of the IPO, but in the wake of

---

14   F. Lavington, *The English Capital Market* (Methuen & Co. Ltd., 1921).

15   R.C. Michie, *The London Stock Exchange: A History* (Oxford University Press, 1999).

16   David Chambers and Elroy Dimson have studied the historical development of LSE and provide a good overview of the regulatory and administrative history of IPOs on the LSE over the last century. Chambers and Dimson (2009).

17   This is now called the Purple Book.

Big Bang these listing requirements were drawn up by the Financial Services Authority (FSA) in accordance with the Financial Services Act 1986 (FSA 86).

FSA 86 was replaced by the Financial Services and Markets Act 2000 (FSMA). On 1 May 2000, the responsibility for listing on the Main Market of LSE was transferred from the exchange to the FSA. In the context of listing, the FSA is generally referred to as the UK Listing Authority (UKLA). At this time a distinction between admission to listing and admission to trading was also introduced. In 2013, the FSA was granted bigger powers to champion consumer rights and was renamed as the Financial Conduct Authority (FCA).

2.3 A brief history of IPOs in the UK since 1945

IPOs from 1945 to the end of the 20th century

From the start of the 20th century through to the end of the second world war, there were a number of IPOs on the LSE. However, the listing rules, and the methods and types of listing, were quite different from what we see today. For this reason I discuss here a brief history of UK IPOs since 1945.

In the first few months after the end of the second world war, the IPO activity at the LSE was negligible. However, it soon began to pick up and by the end of 1949 more than 250 companies had conducted an IPO on the LSE. Over the next two decades the number of IPOs continued to grow as the UK economy stabilised.

There were a total of 617 IPOs during 1960–69, a number almost twice that of 1950–59. The 1970s started with reasonable IPO activity, with more than 190 IPOs joining the LSE during 1970–73. However, the turbulent world events of the mid-1970s took their toll on LSE listing activity. The infamous oil crisis of 1973 followed by the stock market crash of 1973–74, in which the UK stock market was particularly badly hit, resulted in just 33 IPOs during 1974–79.

In the following decade, IPO activity was back to its pre-crisis growth levels with nearly 1,000 IPOs joining the LSE from 1980–89. This decade was different from the previous ones in that it saw a large number of privatisations by the Thatcher government.[18] The first firm to be privatised under Thatcher's government was

---

[18]   The first tranche of BP was privatised in 1977, before Margaret Thatcher came to power. This was seen as a start of the privatisations in the UK.

BAE Systems, which first traded on the LSE in February 1981. Over the next eight years, 16 companies were privatised, including giants such as BT, British Airways, Jaguar and Rolls-Royce. In 1989, a large number of utility firms such as Yorkshire Water (later known as Kelda), Severn Trent, Anglian Water, United Utilities and Northumbrian Water were privatised and listed on the LSE on the same day, 11 December.

The early 1990s saw another round of privatisation IPOs with companies like PowerGen, International Power, Scottish & Southern and Scottish Power coming for a listing at the LSE in 1991. Railtrack was another large privatisation – the company listed in May 1996. Most of these privatisation IPOs shared some common characteristics. They were all offered at prices which were considerably lower than their true values (*Investors Chronicle* suggested that the offer prices were at an estimated 13% discount to assets), debts were written off and most of the privatised companies inherited monopolies.

From the investors' point of view, the privatisation of Associated British Ports (ABP) was perhaps the most profitable IPO. At the time of the IPO, the shares were priced at 14p. If an investor bought shares worth £1,000 at the offer price and held on to them for a year after the IPO, the value of their investment would have increased to £2,500, an increase of 150%. For the really long-term investors (those who bought shares in 1983 and, say, forgot about them until 2003) the returns would have been sizeable as every £1,000 that was invested in ABP at the time of the IPO was worth £27,000 by February 2003. This was something of a missed opportunity as only 8,000 retail investors applied for shares in the British Associated Ports' IPO.

The years 1993 and 1994 were hot years, with more than 150 IPOs in 1993 and 210 IPOs in 1994. In fact 1994 was a record year when more than £10bn was raised through IPOs. A large number of these IPOs were of small to medium-sized companies. House of Fraser, Capital Shopping Centres and British Sky Broadcasting Group were some of the large IPOs that came to the market in 1994.

However, in the following year the total number of IPOs coming to the market dropped sharply with only 86 in 1995, raising only £800m. Again, 1996 proved to be a bumper year for IPOs but did not match the records set in 1994. Large IPOs such as that of Thistle Hotels and Orange were the highlights of the year.

The later part of the 1990s saw IPO activity decline quite sizeably with most IPOs being small in size. The only exceptions were those of Thomson Travel Group and THUS, which raised more than £1bn each.

Figure 2.3 shows IPO activity on the LSE between 1946 and 1999.

Figure 2.3 – IPOs on LSE between 1946–99

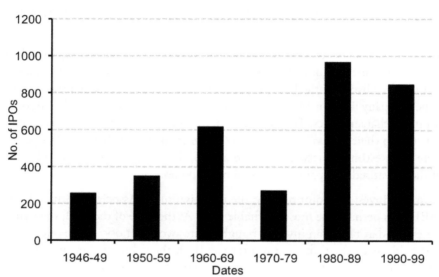

Source: London Stock Exchange 2017.

IPOs since 2000

The first few years of the 21st century could not have been worse for IPO activity. The dot-com bubble burst in 2000 and with it IPO activity went into a deep freeze. Having said that, the year 2000 itself was not a bad year for LSE IPO activity. Even though the dot-com bubble burst in the first part of the year, high tech, dot-com and other types of companies kept on conducting IPOs throughout the year. In total there were 148 IPOs on the Main Market of the LSE, which was more than twice the number seen in 1999.

A large number of these IPOs were from investment and venture capital trusts and other investment entities. Amongst those that drew a lot of media attention were Carphone Warehouse, lastminute.com and EasyJet. The largest IPO in 2000 was that of Granada Media, which came for a listing in July 2000 and raised in excess of £1.3bn. On the first day of trading, shares traded at a 7% premium thus providing the investors a healthy return on their investment.

Over the next three years, IPO activity on the LSE almost stalled with a total of only 32 non-financial IPOs coming to the market from 2001–03. In fact, there were only five non-financial IPOs in 2003, with the Yell Group IPO (a former BT directories business) the only highlight of the year.

The Yell IPO was a global offer (the largest in Europe in 2003) and the company raised £1.3bn. The IPO was considered to be enormously successful as the demand for its shares was overwhelming high, resulting in the company increasing the number of shares on offer by nearly 30%. At the close of the first day of trading, its share price stood at 289.25p thus giving the investors a modest return of 1.4%. However, trading in subsequent days saw Yell's share price fall below the offer price of 285p and it was not until about two weeks after the listing that it rose above the offer price. Yell's share price peaked in 2007 at 600p but by July 2013 had fallen to 0.17p when its shares were suspended from trading and the company collapsed.

Figure 2.4 shows IPO activity on the LSE since 2000.

Figure 2.4 – IPOs on the Main Market of LSE since 2000

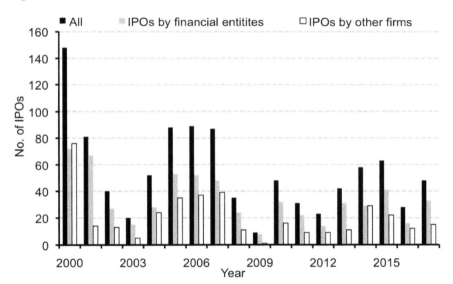

Source: London Stock Exchange 2017.

The start of 2004 saw a renewed interest in IPOs with almost 50 coming to the market during the year. The Halfords and Admiral Group IPOs were the most talked about. Between 2005 and 2007 almost 260 firms came to the market. Large IPOs included Debenhams, Rosneft, Experian and Standard Life.

Debenhams was an unusual IPO in that the company was first listed in 1928 and then again between 1985 and 1998. The firm was taken private by private equity firms CVC Capital Partners, Texas Pacific Group and Merrill Lynch in the year 2003. At the time of the IPO (May 2006), Debenhams saw an oversubscription by two times but still the company priced its share at the bottom of the price band (195p). On the first day of trading the share price rose to 200.25p thus providing the investors with a return of nearly 3%.

Standard Life came to the market in July 2006. Before the IPO, the company was in mutual ownership for around 80 years. Like Debenhams, Standard Life also priced its shares at the bottom of the price band (at 230p). By the close of the first day of trading, investors who sold out would have made a return of around 4.3%.

In 2007, Smurfit Kappa (an Irish paper company) and Sports Direct (the UK's biggest sports retail chain) were two of the largest IPOs that came to the market. Sports Direct was in the news mostly for the wrong reasons. Though the IPO was oversubscribed by nearly three times and was priced at the high end of the pricing band (at 300p), its share price fell by nearly 8% on the first day of trading. Some analysts suggested that this drop in share price was due to plunging Chinese stocks and the fear of a global slowdown. However, the company's woes did not end there. By the end of the first four months of trading, the Sports Direct share price had dropped to almost half of its offering price.

In 2008 and 2009 IPO activity bore the full brunt of a credit crunch and the worldwide financial crisis. In 2008 there were 35 IPOs on the Main Market of the LSE and only eleven of them were from non-financial firms (including life insurance and real estate investment). The largest IPO was from a mining firm Fresnillo Plc, which was an international offering from a Mexican parent company, Peñoles. Perhaps the worst year in the recent history of LSE was 2009, with only one non-financial firm, Exillon Energy, conducting an IPO in December.

In the first quarter of the year 2010, IPO activity on the LSE was higher than that of the whole of 2009. Interestingly, three IPOs came to the Main Market on the same day (24 March). According to the PriceWaterhouseCoopers (PwC) IPO Watch Europe Survey of Q2 (2010), extreme volatility in markets in the year 2010 was creating pricing uncertainty and therefore threatening completion of successful IPOs. Richard Weaver, partner, Capital Markets group, PricewaterhouseCoopers LLP, wrote:

Companies gearing up for a potential IPO in the second half of the year [2010] will be hoping that [the second half of the year] will see some stability return to London and other European markets and produce a more conducive environment for IPOs in the fourth quarter.

Richard Weaver was correct. In the last quarter of 2010 a total of 27 IPOs (non-financial firms) took place at the LSE, a majority of which were on the AIM. Overall, IPO activity at the LSE during 2010 was back at pre-crisis levels. However, there were some noticeable failures and setbacks.

Fairfield, a UK oil company, had to suffer the pain of a collapsed IPO because, even though it was backed by blue-chip investment banks such as Goldman Sachs and Credit Suisse, it could not attract enough investors. Ocado, the online supermarket, barely made it to the LSE. Despite hiring top advisers such as Goldman Sachs, JPMorgan, UBS, Barclays and HSBC,[19] the company had to revise its price range of 200p–275p to 180p–200p and then offer its shares at 180p.

Experts were of the view that the IPO momentum built in the last quarter of 2010 would continue in 2011. Tom Troubridge, head of Capital Markets, PwC, said:

> Barring any unexpected financial or political shocks, the momentum built in the fourth quarter of 2010 should continue into 2011 for Europe's IPO markets. Privatisations will feature in 2011 as European governments take steps to reduce their levels of borrowing. In addition to domestic deals, there should be a return of international transactions into London from emerging economies such as Russia, Kazakhstan and India. A return to the record years of 2006 and 2007 looks unlikely, but 2011 should continue the improving trend seen in 2010.[20]

However, the experts were wrong. 2011 saw a fall in the number of IPOs coming to the LSE's Main Market. Only 31 IPOs were listed during the year, of which just nine were from non-financial firms. Perhaps the highlight of the year was the IPO of commodities trader Glencore International Plc, which came to the market in May. Glencore raised $10bn at admission and was the LSE's largest ever international IPO. It became the first company to enter the FTSE 100 index at admission in 25 years. Glencore chose to list in both London and Hong Kong, and set a price range of 480p–580p per share during the book building period. The company decided to offer its shares at 530p per share. On the first day of trading its stock price closed at 525p. In the subsequent months and years Glencore saw a slow but steady deterioration in its share price. In the middle of January 2016 the company was trading at less than 75p per share. However by

---

[19] Ocado hired a syndicate of eight investment banks. Goldman Sachs, JPMorgan Cazenove and UBS acted as joint sponsors, joint global co-ordinators and joint book runners. Barclays Capital and HSBC acted as co-bookrunners. Jefferies International, Lloyds TSB and Numis Securities acted as co-lead managers.

[20] www.pwc.com

the end of 2017, its share price had recovered and the company was trading in the range of 360p–380p per share which was still substantially lower than the offer price of 530p. By the end of 2018, Glencore's share price had fallen to 290p.

The fall in the number of IPOs coming to the Main Market continued beyond 2011. In 2012 there were only 23 IPOs. The only noticeable IPO was that of Direct Line Insurance Group, a household name in property and casualty insurance in the UK and owned by the Royal Bank of Scotland. The Direct Line IPO was *priced to go* at 175p per share. On its first day of unconditional trading, Direct Line's shares closed at 206p up 18% on the offer price. Direct Line's IPO has also performed exceptionally well in the long run. It was trading above 400p per share in December 2015. Towards the end of 2017 its share price was in the range of 350–370p. As the impact of the financial crisis of 2007–09 began to fade, IPO activity on LSE picked up. 2013 saw 42 IPOs coming to the market, which was almost twice the number of IPOs in the previous year. In the following year, there were 58 IPOs and this number increased to 63 in 2015. Perhaps the most anticipated IPO of 2013 was the privatisation IPO of Royal Mail, the 500-year-old British postal and delivery service group. I will discuss this IPO in greater detail in the next section. 2014 saw a number of IPOs from the general retail, healthcare and banking industries. Most notable amongst these IPOs were those of AA Plc (set up in 1905 by a group of motoring enthusiasts), low cost superstores Poundland and B&M European Value Retail, Spire Healthcare and TSB Bank. Most of these IPOs saw an increase in their share price on the first day of trading, providing investors with an opportunity to make a profit on their investment. However, by the end of 2017 many of these IPOs were trading at a price lower than their offer price. Though the number of IPOs in 2015 was higher than that in the previous two years, most of them were of investment companies such as real estate investment trusts (REITs). This was also the year in which the payment processor Worldpay conducted the largest ever fintech IPO in the UK. On the first day of conditional trading, Worldpay's share price rose from 240p to 265p. By the end of 2017, Worldpay was trading above 410p per share. It was acquired by Vantiv in January 2018.

In 2016, Britain voted on its future relationship with the European Union. In an historic referendum that took place on 23 June that year, people voted for Britain's exit from the EU. Popularly termed 'Brexit', it brought volatility and uncertainty in the IPO market leading to a big fall in the number of firms conducting an IPO on the LSE. There were only 28 IPOs during the year, of which only 12 were from non-financial entities. 34 companies either withdrew or postponed their IPOs and many of these were left out of pocket. For example, PureGym, UK's biggest chain of fitness clubs had two runs at its IPO before abandoning its plans in October. These runs cost the company nearly £6.8m in IPO preparation expenses. In November 2017 PureGym was sold to a US private equity group in a £600m deal.

In 2017, the LSE bounced back from its disappointing performance on IPO listings in the previous year. By the end of the year, there were almost 50 IPOs. There were media reports that some companies were accelerating plans to list before any Brexit deal. The LSE was also vying with the New York Stock Exchange (and perhaps the Hong Kong Stock Exchange) to secure the planned $100bn IPO of oil group Saudi Aramco, the largest company in the world by value. IPOs run on LSE continued in 2018. By the end of the year, there were almost 80 IPOs including one from the luxury carmaker Aston Martin. However, Saudi Aramco IPO remained elusive. If this IPO were to happen, it would be the biggest IPO the world would ever have seen.

2.4 High-profile UK and international IPOs

Even though the IPO activity in the last decade has had its ups and downs, there have been some high-profile IPOs which were widely covered in the financial press. Some of these IPOs were of well-known established firms such as Visa Inc and Royal Mail; while others were of firms such as Facebook, Alibaba and Moneysupermarket, which captured the imagination of investors and the financial press because of their unique backgrounds and business models. It is useful to spend time looking at some of these IPOs to gain an insight into how firms with different types of characteristics and backgrounds enter the IPO market.

The Visa IPO

The USA's largest IPO.

Visa, the San Francisco-based credit card processor, operates the world's largest retail electronic payment network. Before its IPO, Visa was run as a cooperative of some 21,000 financial institutions that issued and marketed Visa credit and debit cards. As a first step towards the IPO, Visa underwent a corporate restructuring by merging some of its international businesses and forming a new company, Visa Inc.

In November 2007 Visa Inc filed its documents with the US regulator, the SEC, for a $17.9bn IPO. The price range within which investors were asked to bid was $37–$42. The IPO was co-sponsored by JPMorgan and Goldman Sachs.

A syndicate of 17 underwriters and several smaller banks was formed by the sponsors. A total of 406m shares were on offer, with the underwriters offering an option to sell another 40.6m (this is called a Greenshoe option, about which there will be more detail in the next chapter).

Even though Visa is a large company, it still acknowledged certain risks to investing in its shares. These risks were mentioned in the listing prospectus and were primarily related to some 50 lawsuits for alleged overcharges, anticompetitive practices lawsuits by American Express and Discover, and some general risks such as higher costs for the company in the event of increasing regulatory scrutiny and the potential risk of further consolidation in the banking industry, which could shrink the market for Visa Inc.

The demand for Visa shares was quite high and the IPO was oversubscribed. As is usually the case with US/UK IPOs, the basis of the allocation of shares was not disclosed by JPMorgan and Goldman Sachs, the lead underwriters of the IPO. The underwriters also did not disclose the number of shares that were set aside for retail investors. Given the oversubscription, the shares that were offered to the institutional investors were rationed and some small investors did not get any shares at all.

Visa priced its share at $44 on 18 March 2008. The price was set above the price band of $37–$42. This above-the-range price was a reflection of the strong interest shown by investors and helped the company to raise an extra $2 per share when compared with the top of the book building range ($42). This meant the company raised an extra $812m from the IPO. Altogether the IPO was a great success with Visa raising $17.9bn, making it the largest IPO by an American firm in the history of the US.

On 19 March 2008, Visa started to trade on NYSE Euronext. At the end of the first day of trading, the share price stood at $56.50. For those who were lucky enough to get some shares, this meant that the first day return on their investment was around 28%.[21] During the day, the share price had risen to above $60 before it settled in the afternoon. The spike in the share price during the morning trading session was because of a strong demand, perhaps by investors who failed to get any or a reduced number of shares during the offer. A large number of initial investors also sold their shares at this time (a practice known as flipping). Nearly 175m shares changed hands on the first day of trading.

Even though Visa came to the market at the height of the financial crisis of 2007–09, its share price in the first few years after the IPO did quite well. In April 2010 its shares were trading at an all-time high of $90. Visa's success on the stock market has continued beyond the financial crisis. By the end of 2017,

---

[21] This does not reflect the transaction costs incurred while selling the shares.

Visa was trading at $116 per share. We will discuss Visa's long-run share price performance in Chapter 4. Figure 2.5 charts the share price performance of Visa since its IPO. In the figure you will notice that the starting share price of Visa is around $14. This is because on 19 March 2015, Visa did a 4-for-1 split in its shares. This means that for each share held pre-split, the shareholder held four shares after the split. When a company splits its shares, the market capitalisation of the company remains unchanged. After the split shareholders own more shares but the shares are valued at a lower price.

If you had invested $10,000 in buying Visa shares at the offer price, continued holding the shares till the end of 2017 and reinvested all the dividends received, your investment would be worth nearly $84,000 over this ten-year period.

Figure 2.5 – Share price performance of Visa IPO (adjusted for share split)

The Google IPO

An IPO that used a Dutch auction.[22]

In the world of IPOs, the Google IPO is known more for its unconventional nature than for the notability of the firm itself.

From its humble beginnings in a garage in California in 1998, Google grew into a business with a turnover of around $1.47bn by 2003. Towards the later part of 2003, Google announced that it had decided to go public and would come to the market in the following year. The owners decided it was now the right time to tap the benefits of listing on a stock market, both for the firm and its initial shareholders.

On 19 August 2004, Google went public on the NASDAQ, pricing its shares at $85 each and selling in excess of 19m shares. Interestingly, the company used an uncommon approach for the listing; namely a modified *Dutch auction*.

Before we go any further, let's look at what exactly a Dutch auction is and how it differs from the more conventional *firm commitment* IPO method.

How firms are valued for IPOs: firm commitment and Dutch auctions

As will be discussed in the next chapter, one of the most important aspects of the IPO process is the valuation of the issuing firm. Traditionally, in the US, firms have used the firm commitment method to price their shares and list on a stock exchange. Under this method, the sponsor plays a crucial role when it comes to the pricing of the firm's shares. In the past, a firm commitment involved the setting of the share price of a company (by the sponsor) and the investors then being asked to subscribe to the shares. Since the early 1990s, the firm commitment involves a book building exercise where the company (with the help of the sponsor) comes up with an indicative price range of its shares. Investors are then asked to submit their bids so that the company builds a book. Once the book is closed, the clearing price is determined and allocations are made (but these are hardly ever pro rata).

A Dutch auction is another type of price discovery mechanism, whereby potential investors make bids for the shares of a company that is making an IPO at a price of their choice. Once the auction closes, the bids are arranged in descending order of bid prices. The clearing price is then set – usually the highest price at which the firm can sell all its pre-specified number of shares. An interesting feature of this auction is that all those who had submitted their bids above the clearing price still pay the clearing price. If the issue is oversubscribed

---

[22] A large part of the discussion is taken from my article, 'The Google IPO: An Analysis', *Journal of Management Case Studies* (ICFAI) (2005), pp. 36–38.

at the clearing price then shares are allocated to the winners on a pro rata basis.[23] The major difference between a book-built firm commitment and a Dutch auction is that in the Dutch auction, the sponsor does not have any say in the pricing of the issue or in the allocation of the shares to potential investors.[24]

*   *   *

One wonders why Google chose to use a Dutch auction, which is an especially uncommon IPO method for a large listing. The owners of Google said that they wanted ordinary small investors to participate in the issue and therefore a Dutch auction would be ideal. However, if wider participation was the goal then using the firm commitment method and asking the sponsor to use a pro rata allocation that does not differentiate between institutional and individual investors might have been more suitable. Moreover, if Google wanted the participation of small investors they could have given these investors equal voting rights; but instead of doing this the owners of Google came up with a system of dual classification of shares, with different voting rights, and made sure they had control over the firm after the listing. Considering all of this, it may be that a Dutch auction was used because its cost to the firm is much lower than that of a firm commitment.

The Dutch auction used by Google led to the IPO being severely criticised for three main reasons:

- it encountered a number of regulatory and stock market challenges during the IPO process,

- it was forced to lower its initial price range from $108–$135 per share to $85–$95 per share, and

- it failed to involve small investors because of the complexity of the process.

More specifically, Google was criticised for breaking the quiet *period* rule of the SEC,[25] for the failure to disclose shares allocated to employees and consultants (the dual share classification) and, more fundamentally, for the unconventional method chosen for going public.

The criticism is not well founded though. The controversies regarding the quiet period, allocation of shares etc., could have been levelled even if Google chose the firm commitment process. The lowering of the share price range could also

---

23 The winners of the auction get allocations in equal proportions of their initial bids.
24 See Bill Mann, 'Going Dutch with Google', 26 May 2004 (www.fool.com).
25 Quiet period is where the firm conducting the IPO is subject to an SEC ban on promotional publicity. Google allegedly broke the quiet period rule by speaking about its IPO to a magazine.

have happened even with a firm commitment, if the demand in the market was not strong enough.

To some extent small investors were left out (because not all investors would be able to go through the complexities of the Dutch auction), but comparatively speaking the participation of small investors was much higher in the Dutch auction than it would have been in a firm commitment, under which system the sponsors have the option to pick and choose which investors to allocate shares to.[26]

Further, if a firm commitment was used, the sponsor would have tried its best to set the offering price as low as possible for at least two reasons. First, the sponsor could allocate highly underpriced shares to its chosen customers. Second, by underpricing the shares, the underwriter would have minimised the risk of an under-subscription. If the share price had been set much less than $85, then the effective *money left on the table* – the underpricing – would have been much larger, thus leading to a potential loss to the firm and its owners. For the investors who were lucky enough to get allocations, a 20% return on the first day of trading is quite reasonable looking at historical levels. If a firm commitment were to be used, small investors would have stood no chance whatsoever of getting a fair allocation of shares.

In sum, Google's IPO performance was optimal for both the owners and the investors.

Given that Google faced these issues and it came to list when the market was cold towards IPOs, its listing can be considered a success. The share price jumped to around $100 during the first day of trading, thus giving a *first day pop* of about 18%.[27] This 18% leap was impressive, but was quite conservative when compared with the performance of other tech firms during the dot-com boom – in the period 1999–2000 internet companies gave an average first day pop of around 89%.[28]

From the time of the IPO until the end of 2007 Google's share price steadily rose, until it reached its highest level of $714 in December 2007. It was partly because of the surge in its share price that Google was able to overtake Time Warner to become the world's largest media company. By the end of December 2018, Google's shares were trading at slightly above $1,000. Figure 2.6 charts the share price performance of Google since the time of its IPO.

---

[26] For details of a Dutch auction see WR Hambrecht & Co at: www.openipo.com/ind/index.html

[27] A first day pop is called underpricing in IPO literature.

[28] Ljungqvist and Wilhelm 2003.

Figure 2.6 – Share price performance of Google IPO (adjusted for share split)

The Alibaba IPO

The world's largest IPO.

On 19 September 2014, Alibaba, China's largest ecommerce company conducted the biggest IPO in history. Alibaba raised $21.7bn by selling more than 320m shares by listing on the New York Stock Exchange (NYSE). In a 442-page IPO prospectus filed with the US Securities and Exchange Commission (SEC), Alibaba provided details of the IPO, its history, risk factors, accounts and other pieces of information usually contained in a listing document. A syndicate of 19 investment banks and financial services firms underwrote the IPO.

Alibaba was established in 1999 under the leadership of Jack Ma, a former English teacher from Hangzhou, China. The company's founders shared a belief that the internet would allow small and medium sized firms to grow and compete in domestic and international markets. Alibaba provides an online platform where both small and large merchants can sell their products. However, unlike Amazon, Alibaba does not directly sell or ship items to customers.

Alibaba's listing prospectus didn't include much about why the company was doing an IPO and how it planned to use the money raised – all $8.25bn of it. In the use of proceeds section of the IPO prospectus, the company declared: "We plan to use the net proceeds we will receive from this offering for general corporate purposes". However a quick look at pages 112–116 of the IPO prospectus shows that over a period of three to four years leading to the IPO, Alibaba was making a number of strategic investments and acquisitions, both in China and abroad, to expand its user base and add complementary products and technologies. Perhaps Alibaba planned to continue further acquisitions in future and for that it needed a lot of capital which an IPO can provide. Another reason for the IPO was that principal shareholders such as Jack Ma and Yahoo wanted to sell some of their holdings in the company. Indeed, of the 320m shares sold in the IPO, 123m were primary and the remaining 197m were secondary.

At the time, Alibaba was seen as the most anticipated IPO of the 21st century with its fair share of controversies. Jack Ma's first preference to list his company was the Stock Exchange of Hong Kong (SEHK). This was primarily because of Hong Kong's proximity and shared culture and language with mainland China. Alibaba is run through a *partnership governance* structure, which can be seen as similar to a *dual-class* share structure. However, HKEx listing rules don't allow for such ownership and control structures. Firms listed on HKEx strictly follow the 'one share, one vote' policy. Alibaba insisted on maintaining its partnership governance structure. But HKEx did not budge from its principled stand. Ultimately Alibaba chose to list on the New York Stock Exchange, which allowed it to keep its partnership governance structure. There were other controversies as well. One related to the spinoff of Alipay, the company's payment platform. Alibaba had to update its listing prospectus to clarify the information provided in an earlier filing of the prospectus.

Alibaba kicked off its road show in the week beginning the 8 September 2014. The initial expected price range of $60–$66 was soon increased to $60–$68 because the IPO was quickly oversubscribed. A day before its listing, Alibaba priced its share at $68. The opening price on the first day of trading was $92.70. By the close of the first day of trading the share price was $93.89, a jump of 38% from the offer price. More than 270m shares changed hands on the first day of trading. However from the second day onwards, Alibaba's share price started to fall and it continued to do so for the next four weeks. After a brief period of recovery, the share price continued to fall again. By the end of the first year of trading, Alibaba was trading at $57.39, almost $10 below the offer price. But then came a phenomenal turnaround. After a brief period of volatility at the end of 2015, Alibaba's share price began to rise. This trend continued throughout 2016 and 2017. In late 2018, Alibaba was trading at $150 per share. Figure 2.7 charts the share price performance of Alibaba since the time of its IPO.

In sum, Alibaba's IPO has been a success, both for the company and its investors. Those who sold their shares on the first day of trading made huge gains. After a brief period of volatility in the share price, long-term investors have also been winners. The Alibaba IPO also shows that companies do not necessarily need to list in their home countries. They can be very successful on a foreign stock exchange, too. They need to dream big and prepare well.

Figure 2.7 – Share price performance of Alibaba IPO

The Admiral Group IPO

An IPO that sold only secondary shares.

The UK car insurance group Admiral was launched in January 1993 with just 57 employees, one brand and no customers. By the end of December 2009, it had 3,500 employees around the world, 13 brands and over two million vehicles insured.

In November 1999, Admiral Group's CEO, Henry Engelhardt, performed a management buyout (MBO) from the Brockbank Group. Barclays Private equity backed the deal by investing £20m in the MBO.

In September 2004, Admiral Group conducted an IPO on the LSE. This IPO was interesting in that all the shares were sold by the existing shareholders and no shares were sold on behalf of the firm (primary shares). In other words, the IPO was made up only of secondary shares; a characteristic that is not too common in the IPOs that list at the LSE.

So, even though Admiral did not need capital – owing to the cash-generative nature of its business – it decided to conduct an IPO so as to provide its private equity shareholders (Barclays Private Equity and XL Capital) a chance to sell their holdings in the company. In addition, most of the employees of Admiral were also the shareholders of the company and an IPO would also provide them an opportunity to consume some of their capital tied up in the firm.

Admiral hired Merrill Lynch International as the global coordinator, book runner and sponsor to the IPO. The company used the book building[29] method to arrive at the IPO share price. A price range of 245p–300p was set and potential investors were asked to submit their bids. A total of 84.1m shares were on offer, which accounted for 32.5% of the ordinary share capital of the firm.

By the close of the book building exercise, an order book of £1.5bn was generated, showing that the IPO was oversubscribed by seven times. UK institutional investors dominated the book with 75% of the bids made by this group. US investors took around 20% of the deal and the remaining 5% was taken by European investors.

Based on the information accumulated during the book building, Admiral's shares were priced at 275p each, thus valuing the firm at more than £710m. This raises the question of why Admiral did not price its shares at the top end of the book building range (300p), given the high level of oversubscription for its shares in the market. While the details of the book are almost never made public, one reason that a company might do this is that they have chosen to purposely sell the shares at a discount – a process known as underpricing. (I will discuss underpricing in greater detail in subsequent chapters.)

Before the IPO, 39% of Admiral's shares were owned by its management, 33% by Barclays Private Equity, 14.5% by Munich Re, 8% by employees and 5% by XL Capital. All of these shareholder groups (except Munich Re) sold all or a part of their stake. Apart from the CEO, a windfall was seen by the employees and Barclays Private Equity. If all the 8% of the shares in employee hands were to be sold at the time of the IPO, each employee, on average, would have made nearly £37,000 (which the CEO Engelhardt said "would not be life changing but enough to buy a new car"). As for Barclays Private Equity – for every £1 they invested at the time of the MBO, they received £15 at the time of the IPO.

The year 2004 was not a particularly good year for IPOs as a number of flotations were cancelled due to a lack of investor demand, and market analysts were not too kind with their views on the Admiral IPO. Some were of the opinion that the company had overestimated its value and that there was no reason for it be conducting an IPO in the first place, as it was not raising any cash through

---

[29] More discussion on this and other methods of listing later.

the IPO. Others thought that it was difficult to value Admiral as there were no similar listed companies and that Admiral was drawing its revenues from three streams: brokerage, underwriting and profit commissions. All these doubts were laid to rest when Admiral successfully conducted its IPO on 23 September 2004. On the first day of trading, the share price closed at 287p, which was 4.4% above its offer price of 275p.

From the time of its IPO, the share price of Admiral climbed continuously to touch a high value of nearly 1750p in June 2011. This was an incredible performance given the volatility of the markets in the period. After a rough second half of 2011, when the share price fell by almost half, Admiral has continued to be a good long-term investment. At the end of 2018, Admiral was trading at around 2000p per share. Figure 2.8 charts the share price performance of Admiral since the time of its IPO.

Figure 2.8 – Share price performance of Admiral IPO

The Moneysupermarket IPO

An IPO where the share price did not perform well on its initial trading day.

Entrepreneurs Simon Nixon and Duncan Cameron set up Moneysupermarket (www.moneysupermarket.com) in 1998 as a mortgage search and comparison website.[30] Over the next few years, the company expanded rapidly by including more products such as comparisons on credit cards, personal loans, insurance and travel in its portfolio of services.

The business came for an IPO in the middle of 2007 with Credit Suisse as its global coordinator, book runner and sponsor. The IPO was the biggest worldwide internet company flotation since Google's IPO in 2004. Like Admiral Group, Moneysupermarket also chose to list on the Main Market of the LSE and used a book building exercise to price its shares. The range in which share applications from prospective investors were invited was 170p to 210p.

There were two main differences between the Admiral Group IPO and the Moneysupermarket IPO:

1. With Admiral, no new shares were created and sold at the time of the IPO, whereas in the Moneysupermarket case both the firm and the existing shareholders sold shares. The ratio was roughly half and half: a total of 105.8m shares were sold on behalf of the firm (primary shares) and another 109.2m were sold on behalf of the existing shareholders (secondary shares). This represented 43.4% of the company's enlarged ordinary share capital and raised nearly £366m. *Remember that there is no technical difference between primary and secondary shares from the point of view of the new investor in the firm.*

2. In the case of the Admiral Group IPO, shares were only sold to institutional investors whereas in the Moneysupermarket IPO both institutional and retail investors were invited to apply for shares. CEO Simon Nixon said: "Our advisers said, 'Don't do a retail offering, it's a pain.' We said, 'No, we want to do one. We want to be a consumer champion'."[31]

So serious was the firm about involving retail investors in its IPO, it set up a dedicated retail share offer IPO website. This website aimed to help retail investors understand more about the company, the IPO process and to register for shares. Those who were quick to register an interest in the shares of the company were to receive a discount on the shares.

The tactics Moneysupermarket used in its IPOs make sense when you consider the business of the company. Engaging retail investors in the IPO was a sensible move because the company was trying to become the favourite destination of anyone wanting to compare prices on the internet. Thus, the more noise it made

---

[30] The group was initially established as an offline business in 1993. Using its business-to-business mortgage sourcing experience, the group launched Moneysupermarket, offering its customers the opportunity to search and compare mortgages online.

[31] *Daily Telegraph.*

about its share issue, the more people would remember it when searching to renew their insurance.

From the sale of its new ordinary shares, the company received net proceeds of £170m. A large part of this was used to repay existing debt[32] and the remaining amount was to be used for the company's expected growth. After the IPO, Simon Nixon and other senior managers owned a majority stake in the company and agreed not to sell any more shares[33] for a period of three years after the IPO.

On 26 July 2007, conditional trading[34] of the company's shares began. At the close of the first day of this conditional trading the share price of Moneysupermarket stood at 158p, 7% below its offer price of 170p. On the first day of unconditional trading (31 July 2007), the share price opened at 165p and closed at 169.5p. This meant that all the investors who were allocated IPO shares would have suffered a loss if they had sold their shares on the first day of trading. In fact the share price did not reach the 170p level until two months after the IPO.

There could be a number of reasons why the Moneysupermarket share price performed badly:

1. It may have been bad luck, or at least bad timing. The market at the time of the IPO was showing a shrinking appetite for IPOs of risky companies in the light of growing fears of a credit crunch. The day on which Moneysupermarket started to trade conditionally was the day on which the main LSE indices dropped by more than 3%, the biggest one-day percentage fall in four years. A week before the listing, banks were confidently expecting a price closer to 200p. In reality the company wanted to float several months before it actually did. However, a lack of agreement between the two co-founders delayed the process. Simon Nixon told the press: "I suppose we have been a bit unlucky, but the really positive thing for us is that we have been able to get our flotation going at all. It shows a lot of interest from investors."[35]

2. There were some concerns about the company itself. These concerns ranged from low barriers to entry to general scepticism about founder-led IPOs following the issues with the Sports Direct IPO earlier in the year.[36] In the

---

[32] Simon Nixon bought the 45% stake of the co-founder Duncan Cameron for £162m. This was financed through debt which was to be paid off from the proceeds of the IPO.

[33] This is termed as a lockup or a lockin agreement. More on this later in the book.

[34] Some IPOs have a conditional and then an unconditional trading. Conditional trading takes place before the official listing on the Stock Exchange and is therefore seen as off-exchange trading. More on this in the next chapter.

[35] *Financial Times.*

[36] Sports Direct conducted its IPO in March 2007. The founder Mike Ashley sold

year before the IPO, the company had a profit of £11.7m. Analysts argued that with such a small profit figure the company could not command a valuation of nearly £1bn.

In September 2007, in its maiden set of financial results as a quoted company, Moneysupermarket showed strong revenue growth and saw its share price rise above the offer price for the first time since the IPO. It touched 215p in October 2007. However, over the next 18 months Moneysupermarket saw a sustained decline in its share price. In March 2009, its shares were trading below 35p. But then came a phenomenal turnaround in the company's fortunes. On the back of a sustained year-on-year increase in revenues and operating profits, Moneysupermarket's share price has consistently risen over the last eight years. By the end of 2018, it stood at 280p. Figure 2.9 charts the share price performance of Moneysupermarket since the time of its IPO.

Figure 2.9 – Share price performance of Moneysupermarket IPO

47% of his stake in the business for nearly £930m. The shares were reduced to half their value in the first four months of trading. Mike Ashley was accused of failing to give proper information to investors (Source: *Evening Standard*, 26 July 2007).

The Facebook IPO

An IPO by the world's largest social networking company.

On 18 May 2012, Facebook started trading on NASDAQ with an offer price of $38 per share and a ticker symbol 'FB'. Trading on NASDAQ opens at 9:30am but IPO firms that list on NASDAQ can choose to start trading at a later time. Facebook had planned an 11:00am start but it was not until 11:30am when trading in its shares started. The first trade that came in at 11:30am was at $42.05. In the first 30 seconds of trading, more than 80m shares changed hands. By the end of the first day of trading, FB's share price stood at $38.23 and around 573m shares had been traded – making Facebook the most traded IPO on the first day of trading in the US ever. At the time, Facebook's IPO was the third largest in the history of US IPOs (and fifth largest in the world) with the company raising around $16bn. However, the financial press considered it to be a spectacular flop, especially in the short-run.

In 2004, Mark Zuckerberg launched Thefacebook.com as a Harvard social networking website. Soon the website was being used by all universities across the US. By 2006, anyone who was older than 13 and had a valid email address could use Facebook for free. Facebook was incorporated in 2004 and entrepreneur Sean Parker became the company's first president. Venture capitalist Peter Thiel was the first angel financier of Facebook. He invested $500,000 in the summer of 2004, and in return owned 10.2% of the company. Facebook dropped 'the' from its name after purchasing the domain name facebook.com in 2005. Over the next seven years, Facebook's membership grew at an enormous rate and by mid-2012, Facebook had more than 900m registered users around the world. During this growth phase Mark Zuckerberg rejected several takeover attempts including offers from Yahoo and Google, but did receive funding from companies and private investors such as Goldman Sachs, Microsoft and Hong Kong businessman Li Ka-Shing.

As Facebook's membership grew over time, so did the number of initial shareholders. Facebook also started issuing restricted stock units (RSUs) to its employees. These RSUs could not be sold privately before an IPO. Over a period of time, employees were becoming restless as some of them wanted to realise their paper wealth. Some of the initial investors wanted to exit and Facebook was looking for additional debt financing at a time which could not be worse – the height of the financial crisis in 2009. All of these factors played a role in nudging Facebook towards an IPO.

On 1 February 2012, Facebook announced plans for its IPO by filing Form S-1 with the US Securities and Exchange Commission (SEC). Heavyweight investment banks Morgan Stanley, JPMorgan and Goldman Sachs were appointed as lead underwriters to the IPO. In early May, the initial price range for book building was announced as $28 to $35 and nearly 337m shares were being offered in the IPO, of which 180m were primary and the rest were secondary shares. Facebook did its road show in the second week of May. On 15 May, three days before the IPO, Facebook increased its price range to $34–$38 and increased the total number of shares offered to 421m. The final offer price was decided to be the upper end of the new price range at $38 per share. Many commentators, analysts and even academics were of the view that at $38 per share, Facebook was substantially overpriced.

On the first day of trading a record number of Facebook shares exchanged hands but the usual jump in share price commonly seen in IPOs was surprisingly absent. Though the share price did touch a high of $45 during the day, it closed at just 23 cents above the offer price of $38. It is rumored that Facebook's underwriters spent almost $66m in preventing the company's share price from falling below the offer price. This price support is legal and comes about when underwriters use their own money to buy shares in the open market thus helping to stabilise the falling share price of an IPO company. These underwriters had agreed at a much lower 1.1% underwriting fee (the usual fee could be anywhere from 3% to 7%) because they all wanted to be associated with such a prestigious IPO. However Facebook became a winner's curse that cost them almost 40% of their underwriting fee in providing price support.

If the first trading day was bad from the share price performance point of view, the next day was worse. From the second day of trading, Facebook's share price went into freefall. On the 4 September 2012, Facebook was trading at its all-time low of $17.73, 54% below its offer price. But since then, Facebook's stock market performance has risen like a phoenix. By the summer of 2013, its share price was close to the offer price of $38 and there has been no looking back since. In the middle of 2018, FB was trading around $200 per share. All those who believed in the future of the company and who have been long-term investors have been adequately compensated by the rising share price. Facebook's IPO has turned out to be a 'no first-day pop but a long-run top' investment for many. Figure 2.10 charts the share price performance of Facebook since the time of its IPO.

Figure 2.10 – Share price performance of Facebook IPO

The Royal Mail IPO

An IPO that privatised UK's postal service.

After a few hundred years of government ownership, Royal Mail, the UK's leading provider of postal and delivery services, listed on the London Stock Exchange on the 15 October 2013. Though the origins of Royal Mail date back nearly 500 years to the time of King Henry VIII, it was not until 2007 that an independent review of the postal services sector commissioned by the government recommended the divestment of Royal Mail from public ownership. Divestments of state owned enterprises (known as privatisations) commonly happen through IPOs. On 12 September 2013, the government announced its intention to proceed with a Royal Mail IPO.

Most of the UK privatisations took place during the 1980s and 1990s, so Royal Mail was the biggest government flotation for two decades. As was the case with most of the privatisation IPOs, Royal Mail's took place through a public offer. This meant that both private and institutional investors were allowed to apply for shares. We will discuss the different methods UK companies use to conduct their IPOs in the next chapter.

More than 521m shares were offered in the IPO. All of these were secondary shares, so no new money was raised for Royal Mail through the IPO. Initially the book building price range was set between 260p–330p per share. This was later revised to 300p–330p in early October. Top investment banks including Goldman Sachs International, UBS, Barclays and Bank of America Merrill Lynch were given the lead role in the syndicate. The Royal Mail IPO was very well covered by the financial press and there was a sense of euphoria at the time of book building (mostly because small and private investors were also being allowed to apply for shares). By the close of the application deadline on 8 October, nearly 700,000 applications had been received from individual retail investors. In an official news release on the 10 October 2013, the then business secretary, Vince Cable made a detailed announcement about the Royal Mail IPO. Some of the important highlights of the announcement included:

- The offer price has been set at 330p per ordinary share.

- Based on the offer price, the total market capitalisation of Royal Mail at the commencement of conditional dealings will be £3.3bn.

- The offer comprises 521.7m existing ordinary shares, excluding over-allotment arrangements (the base offer), representing 52.2% of Royal Mail's share capital on admission.

- Total gross proceeds raised in the offer will be approximately £1,722m assuming no exercise of the over-allotment option and £1,980m assuming exercise in full of the over-allotment option.

The original announcement was 11 pages long, but the summary above offers an insight into the level of detail and transparency provided in this particular IPO. Such details, especially on share allocation, are highly desirable but almost unheard of in European and North American IPO markets.

Royal Mail chose to start trading on the London Stock Exchange's grey market (we discuss grey markets in Chapter 3) on the 11 October 2013 under the ticker RMG. Unconditional dealings began at 10:00am on the 15 October with an opening share price of 478p. By the end of the day, shares were trading at 489p – a jump of nearly 48% on the offer price. Within a week, shares were trading at 550p. As the early sellers were making a killing on their investments, criticism of government's handling of the controversial flotation grew. There was a public outcry and the opposition Labour Party accused the government of selling a prime state asset on the cheap.

It soon emerged that at the time of the beauty parade, to select potential underwriters at least two investment banks had proposed a 500p price for Royal Mail's IPO. Neither of these two banks was selected for the IPO which the government priced at 330p. Lazard & Co, which acted as a financial advisor to the government on the IPO, was grilled by MPs as it was Lazard that had advised the government not to increase the offer price of the shares from 330p.

Interestingly Lazard followed its own advice and bought six million shares at the offer price (which the company sold within 48 hours at 470p making a profit of £8.4m). Margaret Hodge, chair of the parliamentary public accounts committee (PAC), said Lazard "made a killing at the expense of the ordinary taxpayer that lost £750m on day one" of Royal Mail's London Stock Exchange debut.

It later emerged that of the 16 priority investors who were given large chunks of Royal Mail shares at the time of the offer, six had sold all their shares in the immediate aftermarket and a further six sold almost all their allocations within weeks. These priority investors were allocated shares to ensure that the new company started with "a core of high-quality investors" who "would be there in good times and bad". The business secretary had promised to marginalise "spivs and speculators".[37]

Within three months of the IPO, Royal Mail's share price touched a high of 615p, after which it began to fall. By October 2014, the share price had fallen to around 390p. This roller coaster continued till the end of 2017. The first six months of 2018 saw Royal Mail's share price touch new heights, trading at around 610p. However, by the end of 2018 the share price had fallen by half to around 300p. Figure 2.11 charts the share price performance of Royal Mail since the time of its IPO.

Figure 2.11 – Share price performance of Royal Mail IPO

37   See 'Royal Mail float scandal: how hedge funds cleaned up', *Independent*, 29 April 2014.

Summary of IPO case studies

A closer look at the IPOs of Visa, Google, Admiral, Moneysupermarket, Alibaba, Facebook and Royal Mail, shows us that the IPO world is not homogenous. Companies come from different backgrounds, both private and state-owned, choose different ways of listing, and make different decisions on the sale of primary and secondary shares. Each IPO, therefore, should be assessed based on its background and characteristics.

Though the Visa IPO came to the market at the time when the sub-prime crisis in the US was unfolding, it was still oversubscribed. Investors who made applications to subscribe to Visa's shares were not deterred by adverse market conditions. They realised (perhaps correctly) that Visa was a sound company worth their investment. Similarly, Google, even with its unconventional listing method, had a successful IPO. Admiral's IPO was only made up of secondary shares, yet it was seven times oversubscribed. It is clear that the worries potential investors may have had about Admiral selling shares only from existing owners were more than compensated by the faith they had in Admiral's business model. Moneysupermarket's IPO shows that hiring a top investment bank (such as Credit Suisse) is no guarantee that the IPO will receive a warm reception from investors. Alibaba chose to leave its relatively safe domestic environment to venture into one of the most advanced IPO markets of the world i.e. the US, and yet conducted a highly successful IPO. Facebook, with all its public appeal, flopped in the short-run but then made a phenomenal turnaround in the long-run. Royal Mail's IPO was highly controversial in that it left a lot of 'money on the table'. Perhaps government privatisation IPOs are meant to do just that.

3

Mechanics of IPOs

In this chapter I discuss the mechanics of an IPO. I start with a look at the different methods of flotation available to UK IPOs and then provide the timetable of an IPO. I also provide a discussion of how underwriters price IPOs by using an example of a hypothetical firm – this is an interesting area and one on which not much has been published. The later sections of the chapter discuss how IPO shares are applied for, how IPO shares are allocated and how IPO shares are traded.

3.1 Methods of flotation

In the UK, a firm planning a listing can choose different methods of conducting an IPO.[38] These methods have different implications both for potential investors and the firms themselves. The two main methods of going public are:

1. Public offer

2. Placing

1. A public offer

In a public offer, the underwriter offers the company's shares to private and/or institutional investors (for example, pension funds and insurance companies) and normally arranges for the offer to be sub-underwritten by a syndicate. A

---

[38]   A large part of this section is based on my paper, 'The Strategy of Going Public: How UK Firms Choose Their Listing Contracts', joint with M. Goergen and R. Mudambi, published in *Journal of Business Finance & Accounting*, 2006.

public offer could be domestic or global. A public offer usually comes with an explicit guarantee from the underwriter that if any shares remain unsold (after the close of applications), the underwriter will buy them from the IPO company.

Within public offers, there are a number of variations:

- In an *offer for sale* (the most commonly used public contract in recent years) the sponsor offers shares at a fixed price to individual and institutional investors. For example, in the largest IPO on the Main Market of the LSE for the year 2008, Fresnillo Plc chose to use a global public offer. It priced its shares at 555p per share and invited subscriptions from investors from a large number of countries around the world.

- In an *offer for sale by tender*, investors are invited to state a price (above a minimum reserve price) at which they are willing to buy. A strike price is then selected at which the shares are offered to investors. The last time this method was used to conduct an IPO was in the mid-1980s.

- An *offer for subscription* is similar to an offer for sale but it is usually only partially underwritten, or not underwritten at all. The companies using this method state at the outset that if the sale of shares does not raise a certain minimum, the offer will be aborted. Here the company (rather than the sponsor) offers shares directly to the public. For example, when Puma VCT 12, a new venture capital trust, conducted an IPO in the summer of 2016, it used an offer for subscription. The front page of the listing prospectus mentioned that the offer was not underwritten.

- In an *intermediaries offer*, the shares are sold to financial intermediaries such as stockbrokers who then sell these shares to their own clients. These types of offers are rare. In fact, according to the LSE, the last intermediaries offer on the LSE was almost twenty years ago by Woolworths Holdings, a South African company that went public in June 1998.

In a public offer, the offer price at which shares are offered to the investors can be arrived at by two methods:

- an in-house valuation of the firm (sometimes termed as fixed-price offer), or

- a book building exercise.

With the *in-house valuation* technique, the underwriter uses techniques such as discounted cash flow (DCF) or peer valuation in order to arrive at the total equity value of a firm considering an IPO. For an explanation of how the DCF technique and the peer valuation (looking at comparable companies) approach work in practice, see 'How IPOs are priced' on p. 64.

With a *book-built* public offer, the sponsor suggests an indicative price range for the issue (this would involve in-house valuation of the firm) and solicits indications of interest from potential investors to build the book. When the book is closed, a clearing price is arrived at, which is the maximum price at which all the shares can be sold. This price then forms the basis of the final offer price at which shares are offered to the public. All those who are successful in receiving shares get them at the same price, irrespective of what price they bid originally.

In the 1990s in-house valuations were still common in the UK even though most of the other continental European countries predominantly used book building.[39] Research on a sample of IPOs from 1992 to 1999 showed that only 20% of UK IPOs used the book building procedure as compared with 92% of IPOs in Germany and 79% of IPOs in France. However, over the last twenty years the book building procedure has become more common in the UK.

2. A placing

A placing usually involves offering an IPO company's shares to a chosen group of institutional investors and does not provide a guarantee such as in a public offer (to buy any unsold shares), as it is not underwritten. If the sponsor fails to place an agreed minimum number of shares then the offering is withdrawn.[40] Over the last few years placings have become more common the UK. However, sometimes IPOs use a mix of placing and public offer for listing. In this case a tranche of the shares on offer is sold to institutional investors (placing) and the remaining shares are offered to the general public (public offer). A good example is of the Royal Mail IPO which carried the following offer details in its prospectus:

> The offer comprises an institutional offer and a retail offer (itself comprising an intermediaries offer and a direct retail offer). Under the institutional offer, the ordinary shares are being made available: (i) to certain institutional investors in the UK and elsewhere outside the US in reliance on Regulation S and in accordance with local applicable laws and regulations; and (ii) in the US, only to QIBs in reliance on Rule

---

39 David Chambers (2009) studied different methods of flotation in UK IPOs after the second world war. He found IPOs between 1960–86 mostly used fixed-price offers instead of tender offers (IPO auctions) despite tender offers leading to substantially lower underpricing. This missed opportunity cost issuing firms (excluding privatisations) between £1.7bn and £3.5bn in real proceeds.

40 Placing agreements also show some variation. For example, the placing agreement of Resolution Limited (IPO on LSE in December 2008), mentioned that the joint book runners and joint underwriters had agreed to buy (if need be) all unsold shares at the placing price.

144A or pursuant to another exemption from, or in a transaction not subject to, the registration requirements of the US Securities Act. Under the intermediaries offer, the ordinary shares are being offered by the selling shareholder to intermediaries in the UK for onward distribution to retail investors located in the UK. Under the direct retail offer, the ordinary shares are being offered by the selling shareholder: (i) to eligible employees on a priority allocation basis; (ii) to retail investors located in the UK; and (iii) to permitted service personnel located in certain jurisdictions outside the UK including, without limitation, in the EEA Passported Jurisdictions, but excluding members of the regular forces located in the US, Canada, Australia and Japan.

Comparing public offers and placings

There are a number of differences between public offers and placings. While a placing involves selling shares to a restricted number of large investors such as institutional investors, a public offer has a wider ownership distribution since it usually involves a large number of private investors. Further, public offers and placings also differ in the manner in which the offer price is set and the shares are allocated.

For fixed-price public offers, the offer price is set before information is acquired about the demand for the company's shares and the share allocation is usually done on a pro-rata basis. The offer price is set about two weeks before the shares first start trading. In a placing, the offer price is set after information acquisition and the shares are allocated to a selected base of institutional investors. The offer price is set about a week before the shares first start trading. It is important to note that there is no formal book building per se involved in a placing.

The risk of under-subscription

For public offers, there is a sizeable risk of under-subscription. The most infamous example of a public offer going wrong is that of British Petroleum (BP). BP's privatisation issue in 1987 was undersubscribed to such an extent that the market picked up less than 50% of the shares on offer. The underwriters and their sub-underwriting syndicate had to buy the majority of shares.[41]

The main reason why BP's issue failed was that the October 1987 stock market crash occurred between the day of price fixing of the issue and that of the first trading. Later in 1991, the public offer of Manchester United was only 50% subscribed.

---

41 The financial press at that time called it 'the flop of the century'. For more details see 'Flop of the century?', *Investors Chronicle*, 23 October 1987, p. 17.

Other well-known firms such as the Daily Telegraph, J D Wetherspoon and MFI all managed to sell less than 50% of the offered shares in their IPOs. Similarly, lesser-known firms such as Anglican, GPA Leasing, Eurocamp and Nursing Home Properties (all of which had their IPO during the early 1990s) also suffered from an under-subscription and had their unsold shares bought by their respective underwriters.

It should not be a surprise that under-subscriptions are common in times of economic uncertainty, such as at the end of the first decade of the 21st century. When Ocado announced an initial book building price range of 200p–275p, only 80% of the shares on offer were subscribed to.[42] Retail subscriptions were below expectations with only a few thousand retail investors placing orders for shares. In order to avoid a failed IPO, Ocado had to sharply cut its offer price range (180p–200p) just hours before the order books closed. By lowering the price range, Ocado was able to sell its shares. If it had failed to sell all the shares on offer, the underwriters to the IPO would have been required to buy the unsold shares.[43]

Public information on the level of under-subscription of placings is hard to find. This is partly because of the lower degree of publicity that these issues receive. However, from time to time information on undersubscribed placings does get published. For example, Arcadia Healthcare, which planned to place £15.8m worth of shares a few years ago, had to abandon its IPO because the required number of shares could not be placed with institutional investors. Similarly, OIS International Inspection had to postpone the impact day of its IPO because its sponsors found it difficult to place all of its shares.[44] In July 2010 Fairfield Energy, an oil and gas explorer, postponed its placing because it failed to find enough institutional investors.

In the wake of the 2007–09 financial crisis, a large number of IPOs were either cancelled or postponed. The UK retailer New Look postponed its planned £1.7bn IPO (using a placing) on several occasions because of its inability to sell its IPO shares to investors. Similarly Travelport, a travel services company, had to call off its £1.2bn IPO (using a placing) in early 2010 despite reducing the offer price. Merlin Entertainments, which owns Madame Tussauds and the London Eye, also pulled its float (no information is available on whether Merlin wished to use a public offer or a placing). More recently, Arqiva, a TV, radio and mobile phone mast company which planned the biggest UK IPO for 2017, pulled its IPO from the LSE citing 'market uncertainty'.

---

42   See 'Ocado IPO book covered at revised range', Reuters, 20 July 2010.
43   See 'Ocado faces retail race to withdraw offers', *Wall Street Journal*, 22 July 2010.
44   For more information on these IPOs see 'Debut postponed', *Investors Chronicle*, 18 December 1992, p. 52.

The cost of a failed IPO

The costs of unsuccessful public offers and placings are typically high in both monetary and reputational terms. In a failed public offer, the underwriter has to pick up the unsold shares. In the failure of the BP IPO, the underwriters and their sub-underwriting syndicate ended up with £7bn worth of unsold shares.

In a failed placing, the issuing firm has to pay the out-of-pocket expenses to the sponsor and suffers other losses such as lost management time and legal costs. IXEurope, an IT firm wishing to list on the LSE, abandoned its placing. Its CEO was later reported to have said in an interview that the failure to float cost the firm £6m in lost management time, legal costs, building costs and morale.[45]

When IPOs fail, both the issuers and the sponsors suffer a negative impact on their reputations because of bad publicity, which is difficult to quantify in monetary terms. Hence, for both public offers and placings, there is a real (rather than just perceived) risk of failure. However, there is a clear difference in terms of who bears the risk of the failure, as for a public offer the risk is borne by the underwriter, whereas for a placing it is borne by the issuing firm itself.

From the investor's point of view

For a private investor looking to invest in an IPO, placings are bad news as they are exclusively for institutional investors. Public offers, some international offers, and hybrids of placing and public offers are the only opportunities where an investor can participate in the IPO. This institutional set-up in the UK has in a sense cut off the private investor from the IPO market and it is no surprise that today nearly 85% of UK companies' shares are in the hands of institutional investors. In a large number of cases, the underwriters advise the IPO company to only focus on institutions as potential investors at the time of the IPO. However, some companies, such as Google, Moneysupermarket and Royal Mail, insist on the inclusion of private investors as potential investors at the time of the IPO. Such choices then lead to either a company conducting a public offer or a placing.

---

[45] This issue had top sponsors such as JPMorgan and Lehman Brothers. The building costs were caused by the fact, that as a result of the failed issue, IXEurope had to cancel three long-term building leases. For more information on this see www.thechilli.com/articles/profiles/people/008_guyWillner.asp

3.2 The timetable of an IPO

The preparations for an IPO can start up to two years in advance but the last 12 months see a lot of hectic activity for companies planning a listing on the Main Market of the LSE (six months in the case of AIM firms). This 12-month period will be the focus of this chapter.

The first steps

For most companies the first port of call to discuss the viability of an IPO is their existing advisers, such as their accountants and solicitors. Based on its discussions with financial advisers, the company then takes the first step towards an IPO by hiring a sponsor (usually an investment bank). Choosing the right sponsor is one of the most important aspects of the IPO process and usually one of the most difficult.

Once the company chooses its sponsor, the IPO process is formally begun at a meeting where the strategy and the timing of the flotation are discussed. One of the main tasks of the sponsor is to evaluate the firm on the basis of its performance and future prospects. For this purpose the sponsor requests a full financial history of the firm along with information on its business and plans for the future.

One of the first tasks of the sponsor is to assess the company's general suitability for a listing in the light of its organisational structure and capital requirements. If the preliminary enquiries are favourable, the sponsor instructs an independent firm of accountants to conduct an audit of the company. A satisfactory report from the accountants paves the way for the sponsor to make a formal proposal to the firm.

The countdown to flotation

Once the sponsor's proposal is accepted by the IPO firm, a provisional timetable for the issue is drawn up. This timetable is a countdown to admission to the stock exchange. Admission day is the day on which an IPO starts trading on the stock exchange.

12 to 24 weeks before admission

This period essentially involves the basic preparation for a flotation so that all the necessary elements are in place. The steps completed during this period usually include:

- Appointment of advisers such as the sponsor, corporate broker, lawyers and reporting accountants. Some companies may also feel the need to hire a public relations consultant at this stage.

- A visit by the sponsor to the company's headquarters to discuss the flotation process in detail with the board of directors.

- An agreement on engagement and detailed instructions with the advisers. The advisers issue administrative documents about the flotation, a realistic timetable will be agreed and the advisers will produce a detailed list of the documents required before the flotation can go ahead.

- An advisers' planning meeting where all the advisers will come together with the directors to discuss the precise structure of the flotation and the proportion of shares to be sold at the time of the IPO. No final decision is taken on these issues in this meeting.

- Due diligence by the reporting accountants so as to put together information on the short and long form reports.

- Preliminary consultations of the sponsor with the LSE and the UKLA about the timetable and to prepare the way for the necessary submissions and approvals.

- Planning on how to market the IPO to potential investors. The lead role is usually taken by the brokers since they are in direct contact with the market itself.

Table 3.1 – Activity 12 to 24 weeks before admission

12–24 weeks before admission	Exchange	UKLA	Firm	Broker	Sponsor	Accountant	Lawyers	PR
Appoint advisers			✓					
Detailed instructions to all advisers			✓	✓	✓	✓	✓	✓
Detailed timetable agreed	✓	✓		✓	✓	✓	✓	✓

Source: London Stock Exchange.

Six to 12 weeks before admission

The pace and intensity of the preparations pick up when the admission is only six to 12 weeks ahead. The steps usually completed during this phase include:

- A review of the problem areas, such as marketing plans, issues raised by the LSE or UKLA, etc.

- Accountants' short and long form report. A first draft of the listing prospectus is also completed.

- The submission of requisite draft documents to the UKLA.

- A meeting with the LSE to discuss the company's business and the ways in which the LSE can help in developing an active trading market following the admission.

- Legal verification, where the lawyers begin the task of confirming every statement in the prospectus, is begun.

- An initial review of pricing issues based on current market conditions.

- Detailed valuation of company assets such as pension funds and property holdings.

- A review of PR presentations to discuss the promotional activity surrounding the flotation.

Table 3.2 – Activity six to 12 weeks before admission

Six to 12 weeks before admission	Exchange	UKLA	Firm	Broker	Sponsor	Accountant	Lawyers	PR
Review of problem areas			✓		✓		✓	
Draft prospectus produced			✓		✓		✓	
Other documents in first draft			✓	✓	✓			
Initial review of pricing issues			✓		✓	✓	✓	
First drafting meetings			✓		✓			
Draft documents submitted to the UKLA		✓			✓			
Initial meeting with LSE	✓		✓		✓			
Review PR presentation			✓	✓	✓		✓	✓
Analysts' presentation			✓	✓	✓		✓	✓

Source: London Stock Exchange.

One to six weeks before admission

Following the feedback from the UKLA the listing prospectus now nears its final form. If the company has chosen to use a book building procedure to arrive at the offer price, it will now issue a pathfinder prospectus which will have a price band included. The company brokers will conduct presentations in the main cities within the country and, if required, around the world, in order to convince potential investors to buy shares in the IPO. This process is usually called a road show.

Other important issues that are dealt with in this period are a review of cash flow and forecasts, a completion of the legal verification and the appointment of registrars who will maintain the share register.

Table 3.3 – Activity one to six weeks before admission

One to six weeks before admission	Exchange	UKLA	Firm	Broker	Sponsor	Accountant	Lawyers	PR
Drafting meetings			✓		✓	✓	✓	
Due diligence on prospectus			✓		✓	✓	✓	
PR meetings and road show			✓	✓	✓			✓
Formally submit and agree on all documents with the UKLA		✓			✓			
Pathfinder prospectus (if required)					✓			

Source: London Stock Exchange.

One week before admission

This is the final week leading to the impact day. Impact day is the day on which the final prospectus (if there was a pathfinder) is issued and advertised to the investors and the flotation is officially announced. This week also sees the pricing of the shares. Once the offer price has been agreed, this information goes into the prospectus which is then submitted to the UKLA for approval. Once the UKLA gives its approval, the next stage is the impact day. Finally, at least 48 hours before admission, the formal application for a listing is submitted to the UKLA. At the same time a formal application for trading is submitted to the LSE.

Table 3.4 – Activity one week before admission

One week before admission	Exchange	UKLA	Firm	Broker	Sponsor	Accountant	Lawyers	PR
All documents completed and approved by the UKLA		✓	✓		✓	✓	✓	
Pricing and allocation meeting			✓	✓	✓			
Register prospectus		✓			✓			
Sign subscription agreement			✓		✓			
Print final prospectus					✓			

Source: London Stock Exchange.

The admission week

This is the week in which the company starts to trade on the stock exchange. In this week share applications are received from prospective investors. If the demand for shares is high, an oversubscription occurs and the company and its sponsor then use a basis of allocation. Traditionally this has been on a pro-rata basis. If the issue is undersubscribed then the underwriters will have to pick up all the unsold shares at the agreed price. This is why the sponsors are referred to as underwriters.

The admission

This is the point at which the company's shares are admitted to trading. The basis of share allotment is agreed and is announced to investors. The listing is officially granted by the UKLA and admission to trading is granted by the LSE. The listing becomes effective and dealing in shares begins.

The admission day is chosen well in advance but the company has the right to request a delay in the admission day. If market conditions are adverse, a large number of IPOs are postponed. However, if a completely unexpected event takes place, there is not much that can be done. The Moneysupermarket IPO is a good example.

Moneysupermarket floated on the LSE on the day when the stock exchange index showed the biggest one day fall in four years. However, at the time of the selection of the listing day (both the LSE and the company have a say on the choice of the listing day), no one had predicted that the listing of the company would coincide with such a fall in the market. At the close of the first day of trading, Moneysupermarket was valued at £783m. Had the company floated a day earlier than it did, predictions were that it would have been valued at around £1bn, which represents a loss of nearly £217m.

Table 3.5 – Activity in the admission week

The admission week	Exchange	UKLA	Firm	Broker	Sponsor	Accountant	Lawyers	PR
Submit 48 hour documents	✓			✓	✓			
Formal application for listing and admission to trading	✓	✓		✓	✓			
Pay UKLA and LSE fees			✓	✓	✓			
Listing and admission to trading granted	✓	✓						
Trading commences	✓							

Source: London Stock Exchange.

Once the trading starts, the investors have their first opportunity to realise their gains. This happens when the trading price is more than the price at which the shares were offered to the investors. In the world of IPOs, investors who sell in the initial aftermarket to capture sizeable gains are called *stags* or *flippers*.

3.3 How IPOs are priced

The pricing of the IPO is one of the most sensitive issues in the whole IPO process. If the company is priced too highly then there is a good chance that the potential investors will not be interested in the firm and the IPO may be a failure. If the price is too low, the cost is borne by the IPO firm in terms of forgone capital.

Pricing an IPO is the responsibility of the sponsor, who is expected to be an expert in arriving at a fair valuation of the firm. Traditionally, two methods have been extensively used in order to value an IPO firm:

1. Discounted cash flow (DCF)

2. Peer valuation or comparable companies method

1. Discounted cash flow (DCF)

According to discounted cash flow (DCF), the value of a company is equal to the sum of its free discounted cash flows, after deduction of the net debt situation. The logic of this method is based on the conviction that the value of an investment is equivalent to the flow of money that the intended investment will generate.

The basic methodology behind this approach is to forecast the net cash flows of the firm, say for the next four to five years, and then discount them using the company's cost of capital in order to arrive at the total value of the firm at the time of the IPO. This approach is based on a number of assumptions and is highly likely to suffer from bias. Nevertheless, it is still one of the basic tools of valuation.

There are a number of steps involved in DCF. They can be summarised as follows:

- **Step 1**: The sponsor uses a reasonable planning horizon (usually four to five years into the future) over which to make forecasts on pro forma statements. These forecasts involve variables such as earnings, working capital changes, capital expenditures, etc., which can be used to estimate *net cash flows (NCF)*.

- **Step 2**: The *weighted average cost of capital (WACC)* of the firm is calculated.

- **Step 3**: An assumption is made on the growth rate of revenues beyond the planning horizon and then the *terminal value* of the firm at the end of the planning horizon is deduced.

- **Step 4**: Having calculated the NCF, WACC and the terminal value of the IPO firm, the sponsor uses a financial formula to calculate the total value of the firm at the time of the IPO. This formula captures the net present value of future cash flows of the firm and also the terminal value of the firm. If we subtract the value of outstanding debt at the time of the IPO then we get the value of outstanding equity. When this is divided by the number of outstanding shares (including the ones to be sold at the time of the IPO), we get the estimated price of the share.

- **Step 5**: If the firm has a target amount to be raised through the IPO then the number of shares to be sold at the time of the IPO and the price at which they will be sold will differ from the estimates obtained in Step 4. The value of equity arrived at (using Step 4) is used to calculate the number of shares to be sold and the price at which they will be sold.

An illustration of the DCF method

Medlock Plc is an IT firm which is at its development stage and wishes to conduct an IPO in the first quarter of 2019. To price Medlock's shares, the sponsor Matthew and Fitzgerald would first need to project the company's free cash flows for a reasonable planning horizon. We will assume that this horizon is from 2019 to 2022. As the company is in its development stage, it is not appropriate to make forecasts beyond three years. Also, the IT sector changes rapidly and forecasts beyond three years become highly speculative.

The estimated cash flow statement for the period December 2019 to December 2022 is shown in Table 3.6.

Table 3.6 – Estimated cash flow statement for Medlock Plc

(In millions)	2019 (Estimate)	2020 (Estimate)	2021 (Estimate)	2022 (Estimate)
Net income	−40.060	−4.957	49.850	113.616
Financial results	1.279	0.879	0.659	0.439
Change in working capital needs	−13.788	−26.390	−45.140	−15.678
Amortisation and depreciation	12.123	16.422	22.328	24.951
(1) Cash flow of operational activities	−40.446	−14.046	27.697	123.328
(2) Cash flow of investment activities	−9.776	−11.182	−20.707	−20.486
Issue costs	−15.000	0	0	0
Proceeds of the public offer	178.500	0	0	0
Loans	−16.424	−5.543	−1.373	−1.220
Financial results	−1.279	−0.879	-0.659	−0.439
(3) Cash flow of financing activities	145.797	−6.422	−2.032	−1.659

Free cash flow is defined as the sum of the net profits and the non-cash costs (such as depreciation, depletion and amortisation, building of provisions, etc.), less the net financial investments (participations), net material investments and net increase in working capital (further called changes in assets and liabilities), the reimbursement of loans and the net payment of dividends to minority shareholders. Based on the estimated cash flow statement, the projected end of the year free cash flows for the period 2019 to 2022 are given below.

Table 3.7 – Projected end of year free cash flows for 2019 to 2022

	2019 (Estimate)	2020 (Estimate)	2021 (Estimate)	2022 (Estimate)
Free cash flow (1) + (2) + (3)	95.575m	−31.650m	4.958m	101.183m

These free cash flows are the company's consolidated projections and are prepared on the basis of the projected productivity and market prospects of the company. A part of this projection is usually developed with the help of consultancy firms specialising in marketing strategy for the sector to which the IPO firm belongs. The issuer and its sponsor usually tend to have conservative estimates.

Let's assume that Medlock chooses a zero growth rate for its free cash flows beyond the planning horizon (2022) in order to remain conservative. This means that the free cash flow in the year 2023 is expected to be 101.183m and the same in 2024 and beyond. This gives rise to perpetuity. Now we need an appropriate cost of capital (discount rate) for Medlock Plc in order to discount the future free cash flows to their present value.

In our example we assume that Medlock does not intend to have any debt in its capital structure. Its discount rate is therefore the cost of equity capital which can be calculated using the capital asset pricing model (CAPM). The CAPM makes it possible to determine a discount rate which is an estimate of the annual yield required for an investment in Medlock Plc shares.

The CAPM is used to calculate the discount rate as follows:

Discount rate = R_f + (β x market risk premium)

R_f is the annual yield of a risk-free investment, that is to say the yield on ten-year government bonds. Let's say that this is 4.25%.

β is the projected volatility of the Medlock Plc shares compared with a stock market (in this case, the London Stock Exchange). The β is obtained by using the highest β among the β of the five listed companies most comparable with Medlock Plc (see Table 3.8).

Risk premium is the annual premium of the yield on an average share investment on the LSE in relation to a risk-free (R_f) investment. Let's assume that the risk premium is 6.07%.

Table 3.8 – Projected volatility (β) of comparable companies

Company	PE (2019)	β(annual basis – daily prices)
Tetrix System	58.4 (12/09)	1.420
Glob-E Software	20.0 (03/09)	1.338
Dotgone Systems	22.5 (12/09)	1.874
Froogle	42.8 (07/09)	1.338
Tora Systems	15.7 (12/09)	0.958

The highest β, that of Dotgone Systems at 1.874, has been used for the valuation of Medlock Plc.

Therefore:

Discount rate = 4.25% + (1.874 × 6.07%) = 15.63% or 0.1563

This discount rate is then used to calculate the current value of all the projected free cash flows of future years (which were displayed in Table 3.6). Calculating the current value of the projected free cash flows is important because of the time value of money, i.e. a Pound Sterling today is not the same as a Pound Sterling in one year's time.[46] The present value of a future cash flow can be calculated using the following formula:

$$PV = \frac{FV}{(1+r)^t}$$

Where PV is the present value of a future cash flow, FV is the future value of the cash flow, r is the discount rate and t is time when the future cash flow takes place. As the firm is conducting its IPO in the first quarter of 2019 (is therefore being priced around that time) and the first cash flow (£95.575m) is calculated at December 2019, the time period used to calculate the discount rate is 9/12, or 0.75 (instead of a year).

Present value of the expected free cash flows for 2019 to 2022:

$$\frac{95.575}{(1.1563)^{0.75}} - \frac{31.65}{(1.1563)^{1.75}} + \frac{4.958}{(1.1563)^{2.75}} + \frac{101.183}{(1.1563)^{3.75}}$$

= £123.18m

As Medlock is expected to have a zero growth rate for its free cash flows beyond the planning horizon (2022), the terminal value of the firm at the end of December 2022 is found by applying the discount rate to the estimated free cash flow for 2022:[47]

$$\frac{101.183}{0.1563}$$

= £647.36m

---

[46] The 'time value of money' is one of the basic concepts of corporate finance. A Pound Sterling today is not the same as a Pound Sterling in one year's time (or in other future periods) primarily because of two reasons. First, inflation eats into our purchasing power. If there is inflation in the economy, what we can buy today for a Pound would need more than a Pound if bought in future. Second, if we had the Pound today we can invest it to obtain a return for ourselves (opportunity cost).

[47] To be conservative we have assumed that free cash flows of Medlock will remain constant beyond 2022. This leads us to a perpetuity of £101.183m every year. The present value of this perpetuity can be found by dividing the expected cash flow per year (£101.183m) by the discount rate of Medlock.

This terminal value of £647.36m needs to be discounted to its present value at the time of pricing Medlock (March 2019). This is done by using the present value formula where the FV is £647.36m, discount rate (r) is 0.1563 and time period (t) is 3.75 years. The current terminal value of Medlock:

$$\frac{647.36}{(1.1563)^{3.75}}$$

= £375.52m

Therefore the total value of Medlock Plc at the time of the IPO:

= £123.18m + £375.52m

= £498.7m

If at the time of the IPO the total outstanding debt of the company is £22.6m then the value of equity is:

£498.7m – £22.6m = £476.1m

Medlock Plc has 35m existing shares at the time of the IPO and plans to sell another 38m at the time of the IPO. Therefore, the total number of shares after the IPO will be:

35m + 38m = 73m

The price per share at the time of the IPO will be:

£476.1m/73m = £6.52

Here we have assumed that Medlock wants to sell 38m new shares at the time of the IPO. If they sell their shares at £6.52 per share, the gross amount raised at the time of the IPO will be:

£6.52 × 38m = £247.76m

If Medlock wanted to raise only £150m at the time of the IPO (target amount) then the number of shares and the price at which they will be sold will differ from the one calculated here. If N is the number of shares to be sold to raise £150m then:

$$\frac{476.1m}{35m+N} \times N$$

= 150m

Solving for N we get: N = 16.10m

So the company has to sell 16.10m shares. The price per share will be:

Price per share =

$$\frac{476.1m}{35m + 16.1m}$$

= £9.32

To summarise, the DCF method is based on a number of assumptions, some of which could be totally random. In this illustrative example, we assumed that the growth rate of the free cash flows after 2022 will be zero and we chose the highest beta of the comparable companies. Had we used different growth rate assumptions or the average beta of comparable companies, we would have obtained different valuations.

2. The comparable firms approach

The comparable firms approach is also used frequently by investment banks when pricing an IPO. The method involves selecting a list of firms comparable to the IPO firm in terms of industry, size, risk, growth prospects and profitability. Valuation multiples such as price-to-earnings ratios (P/E ratios), price-to-sales ratios (P/S ratios) or market-to-book ratios (M/B ratios) are then used to compute the issuer's price per share. For example, using the P/E ratio of comparable firms, the price per share of the issuing firm can be calculated as:

Price per share =

$$\left[\frac{P}{E}\right]_{comparable} \times EPS_{IPO}$$

An illustration of the comparable firms method

Let's continue with our previous example of Medlock Plc. As a first step, the sponsor has to choose a set of comparable firms. This presents the first problem for the investment banks. If Medlock Plc is a single-product firm then it might not be judicious to compare it with companies that have a well-diversified product range. Even if some other single product firms in the same industry can be identified they might not be comparable if Medlock is producing an innovative product.

These are some of the issues that sponsors have to confront when they use the comparable firms method of valuing IPO firms. Let's assume that in the case of Medlock, the sponsor was able to come up with a list of five comparable firms. While calculating the cost of capital for the DCF method above we looked at this set of five comparable firms (see Table 3.8). Their P/E ratios varied from 15.7 (Tora Systems) to 58.4 (Tetrix System).

Once the comparable firms and their financial ratios such as P/E, P/S and M/B have been identified, the next step is to arrive at the appropriate comparable ratio to be used for pricing the IPO firm. There are different ways in which these comparable firm ratios can be used. For example, we could use the average of the comparable firm's P/E ratios or we could use the lowest or the highest P/E ratio among the comparable firms. In this case, let's assume that given the positioning of Medlock, even the lowest comparable firm ratio of 15.7 is on the high side and would produce an over-optimistic valuation of Medlock as a company. For this reason, the sponsor could end up using a P/E ratio lower than 15.7.

Let's say that the sponsor, Matthew and Fitzgerald, chooses an arbitrary P/E ratio of 12.7. This ratio is then applied to the projected earnings of Medlock. Once again there is more than one way in which the projected earnings of the IPO firm can be selected. We can select the projected earnings for the year following the IPO, or we can take the average of the projected earnings over the planning horizon. Obviously these different methods will give different valuations for Medlock.

If we apply the P/E ratio of 12.7 to the projected earnings for the year 2021 (the first year after the IPO when the projected earnings are positive, as shown in Table 3.6) then the future value of the firm (at the end of 2021) will be:

P/E ratio × earnings = 12.7 × £49.85m = £633.10m

This future value when discounted at the cost of capital (15.63%) will produce a present value of:

PVMedlock at the time of IPO =

$$\frac{£633.10}{(1.1563)^{2.75}}$$

= £424.65m

Therefore the price per share is:

Price per share =

$$\frac{£424.65m}{73m}$$

= £5.82

This price is lower than the one estimated using the DCF method. As the estimated prices using the two methods are different, the investment bank may use the arithmetic mean of the estimated prices of the DCF and comparable firms approach to arrive at the final price per share.

Table 3.9 – estimated values per share based upon different methods

Method	Estimated value of the company	Estimated value per share
DCF	£476.1m	£6.52
Comparative method	£424.65m	£5.82
Arithmetic mean of the DCF and comparative methods	£450.38m	£6.17

This price of £6.17 may not be the same as the one at which the shares are offered to investors. For example, the shares may be offered at £4.94 (a discount of 20%). This practice is quite common and is usually referred to as underpricing.

To summarise, the comparable firms method is a commonly used method and has its advantages and disadvantages. It is simpler to use than the DCF method but creates a number of challenges when selecting comparable firms or when selecting the appropriate financial ratios of these firms.

3.4 Applying for IPO shares

The method of flotation chosen by the company affects who can and cannot apply for shares. Those firms which choose placing as their method of flotation automatically exclude retail investors. For example, in November 2017 when Bakkavor Group Plc, UK's biggest hummus producer, conducted its IPO on the LSE, it decided to use placing for its flotation. The offering prospectus declared that shares would only be sold to certain institutional and professional investors.

Firms using a method other than a placing are effectively inviting retail investors to apply for IPO shares. Historically, in the UK, the offering prospectus carried an application form. For example, when Manchester United conducted its IPO in the early 1990s, the IPO prospectus contained an application form. However, the internet came into much wider use throughout the 1990s and it soon became less common for IPO prospectuses to have application forms for share purchases in them.

Nearly a decade after Manchester United's IPO, lastminute.com launched its IPO in March 2000. The listing prospectus was almost twice the size of Manchester United's prospectus but did not contain an application form.[48] Instead, the interested investors were asked to register as lastminute.com subscribers and then download the application form from the company's website. Terms and conditions of application for the retail offering were exclusively mentioned in the listing prospectus. For example, the minimum application amount was £500. Applications in excess of this amount had to be in multiples of £500 and the maximum amount that could be invested by retail investors was £3,000. Multiple applications were not permitted and (unlike Manchester United's IPO) joint applications were not permitted either.

Similarly, the prospectus of SuperGroup Plc, which launched its IPO in March 2010, did not contain an application form. Instead, retail applicants who wished to apply for shares were asked to follow instructions on the company's retail offer website or to get in touch with the company's registrars and receiving agents. Investors could make an online application in addition to a paper application. More recently, in the Royal Mail IPO, both online and hard copy application forms were accepted by the company.

Applying for shares in an international IPO being conducted at the LSE could sometimes be a little different – let us take a look at an example of Air China's IPO.

Applying for shares in an international IPO – an Air China example

When Air China conducted a dual listing in London and Hong Kong, it placed a part of the offering with institutional investors in London (which it described as the international offering) and the remainder of the shares were available to retail investors from the Hong Kong market (which it termed as the Hong Kong public offering). The Hong Kong public offering was divided into pools A and B.

Pool A represented all the applicants with an aggregate subscription price of HK$5m and pool B represented investors with an aggregate subscription price greater than HK$5m. Investors could not apply in both pools A and B or in one pool and in the international offering together. Interestingly, the company reserved the right to use different allocation ratios for the two pools. Multiple applications were not allowed. Investors could apply either using one of the two application forms made available by Air China or by electronic application instructions to Hong Kong Securities Clearing Company (KHSCC), which

---

[48] Manchester United's prospectus was nearly 70 pages long. In comparison, lastminute.com's pathfinder prospectus was 143 pages long.

would allow KHSCC nominees to apply for the Hong Kong offer shares on behalf of the investors.

There were also three further very interesting characteristics of the Air China IPO:

1. While making an application, investors had to pay the maximum offer price of HK$3.10 for each share. If the final offer price (after the book building activity) was lower than HK$3.10, the investors would be eligible for a refund but without any interest.

2. Investors were not only asked to pay HK$3.10 per share but were also asked to pay brokerage of 1%, the Securities and Futures Commission (SFC) transaction levy of 0.005%, investor compensation levy of 0.002% and the Hong Kong Stock Exchange trading fee of 0.005% in full. This meant that investors applying for, say, 2,000 shares had to pay HK$6262.74 at the time of application (instead of just the price of the shares, which was HK$6200).

3. Applications were only accepted between 11:45am and 12 noon, providing an application window of only 15 minutes.[49]

* * *

Another way in which the internet has impacted how some IPOs are sold is that small investors can now apply for shares using online platforms such as the one provided by www.allipo.com or the Hargreaves Lansdown IPO service (www.hl.co.uk). All IPO, which is a part of ADVFN group of companies, provides private investors a gateway to IPO investment. On its website, the company declares that its unique business model pools private investor demand and allows them to participate in an IPO along with institutional investors.

All IPO allows retail investors an opportunity to view new IPO investment opportunities, apply for shares and have their investments confirmed. Usually the IPO investment opportunities available on All IPO are for small and start-up firms. Interestingly, the website mentions that investors can apply for shares both in offers for subscriptions and placings.

Hargreaves Lansdown's IPO service allows retail investors to invest in upcoming IPOs. The company's website provides information on current IPOs such as application deadlines, IPO prospectus, factsheet, offer term and conditions and a key information document. The website provides a clear breakdown of the costs and charges payable to the firm.

---

49 Air China went on to have a very successful IPO. It raised nearly £558m after pricing its shares (KH$2.98) near the top of the pricing range. The Hong Kong Public Offering was oversubscribed by more than 83 times.

3.5 How IPO shares are allocated

The issuer, along with its underwriter, decides on how to allocate shares and who they will be allocated to. If the IPO used the book building procedure to arrive at the offer price, the underwriter will have a list of investors who applied for shares. Similarly, for fixed-price offers, the application forms received by the closing date would reveal the total demand for shares. If there is no oversubscription of shares then all those who applied for shares would receive all the shares they have applied for. For oversubscribed IPOs, the underwriter uses its discretion to allocate shares.

Information on how the shares are allocated to different investors is not always made public. However, some IPO companies do publish this information.

SuperGroup Plc conducted its IPO on the Main Market of LSE on 24 March 2010. The company chose a *placing* and *an open offer* to sell 25m shares. This means that the company sold its shares to both institutional and retail investors. While details of how shares were allocated to institutional investors were not made public, allocations to retail investors, employees, and friends and family were announced on the day of listing. The company announced that the retail offer was oversubscribed and that the company exercised its discretion in determining allocations of retail offer shares. Registered employees were allocated 100% of their application; friends and family were allocated 75% of their application and all other applicants received 48.749% of their application. The minimum application was £250 (and multiples thereof).

In the Royal Mail IPO, shares were allocated to employees, retail and institutional investors. The company made the following announcement:

- Over 99% of Royal Mail's approximately 150,000 UK-based eligible employees will between them receive a total allocation of just over 100m free shares in HM government's offer, representing 10% of Royal Mail's share capital.

- The institutional tranche of the offer was more than 20 times subscribed and the retail offer was approximately seven times subscribed.

- 67% of the base offer has been allocated to institutional investors and 33% of it has been allocated under the retail offer.

- All members of the public who have applied for shares in Royal Mail through the retail offer, up to and including applications of £10,000 will receive an allocation of 227 shares which is equivalent to £749.10 at the offer price. This represents almost 95% of all members of the public who have applied – or over 690,000 people. Those who have applied for shares worth more than £10,000 will not receive an allocation, which is in line with the treatment of larger applications in previous well over-subscribed privatisations.

- All members of the public who submitted a valid application for £750 worth of shares – more than 93,000 people – will have their application met in full.

- In total over 270,000 applicants, (37% of applicants) will receive at least half of the shares they have applied for.

- Only approximately 5% of applicants will receive no allocation.

Recent research commissioned by the FCA finds evidence that underwriters make favorable allocations to investors who provide them with information likely to be useful in pricing the IPO, in particular investors who submit price-sensitive bids, and those who attend meetings with the IPO company before the IPO. Underwriters also favour investors from whom they generate the greatest revenues elsewhere in their business, notably through brokerage commissions. Long-term investors seem to receive more favourable allocations than short-term investors (like hedge funds). There was no evidence of allocation bias against investors who flip their shares shortly after the IPO.

3.6 Trading IPO shares

Investors who are allocated shares in an IPO usually have a choice of receiving their shares as certificates (in paper form) or through a paperless settlement procedure known as CREST. If investors wish to use CREST, their accounts are credited on the day of admission. The share certificates may be posted on the same day or sometimes with some delay.

In Moneysupermarket's IPO, the prospectus mentioned that share certificates would be posted on the day of listing whereas, for SuperGroup, the posting of share certificates was scheduled about a week after the admission date. In principle, investors should be able to trade their shares from the moment trading begins (usually at 8:00am) on the day of admission, as by this time they would know if any shares have been allocated to them.

Sabre Insurance Group mentioned in its IPO prospectus that the offer price and share allocation would be announced at 7:00am on 6 December 2017, the day on which conditional dealings were to begin. Therefore investors knew if they had been allocated shares in the IPO a while before the unconditional dealings began on 11 December 2017. This has also been the practice in the past. For example, applicants in Manchester United's IPO would have known if they had been allocated shares a long time before the date of admission. Manchester United's IPO prospectus carried the following information:

> The application list will open at 10.00am on Friday 31 May 1991 and will close as soon thereafter as Henry Ansbacher may determine. The basis on which applications have been accepted will be announced as soon as possible after the application list closes.
>
> It is expected that renounceable letters of acceptance will be posted to successful applicants on Friday 7 June 1991 and that dealings in the ordinary shares will commence on Monday, 10 June 1991.[50]

Interestingly, prospectuses of some IPOs in the last few years show that retail investors would not know if they have been allocated any shares until a few days after the date of admission. For example, Ocado's prospectus carried the following warning:

> Applicants who purchase or subscribe for ordinary shares should note that dealings in the ordinary shares will commence prior to their share account statements being made available online. Applicants who purchase or subscribe for ordinary shares and who deal prior to their share account statements being made available online do so at the risk of selling ordinary shares for which they will not have received an allocation. Share account statements will be made available online to successful applicants by 4 August 2010.[51]

Ocado began trading in the grey market on 21 July 2010[52] and was to be admitted to LSE on 26 July 2010. According to the warning cited above, applicants would not have known if they had been allocated any shares until almost ten days after the date of admission. However, in the timetable for the offers section of Ocado's prospectus, the company mentioned that ordinary shares would be credited to CREST accounts and the Ocado Share Account on the day of admission, i.e. 26 July, and that shareholders with ordinary shares in the Ocado Share Account would be able to buy and sell ordinary shares from admission.[53]

---

50 Manchester United's IPO prospectus, p. 65.
51 Taken from Ocado Group Plc IPO prospectus.
52 In the UK, shares in IPOs can trade before the firm is formally admitted to the stock exchange. This is called the grey market or 'when issued' dealing. Grey markets are discussed in the next section.
53 Ocado Share Account was a company-sponsored nominee arrangement. More details on this in Chapter 5.

This situation with prospective Ocado IPO investors potentially not knowing whether they had been allocated shares or not until ten days after the admission of the company to the LSE is clearly not ideal. However, though there are some exceptions, the vast majority of IPO investors would know if they have been allocated shares by the time unconditional trading in shares begins.

3.7 The grey market

Shares of the IPO firm are traded on listing day, which is also known as the admission day. However, in the UK IPO shares can be traded before the listing day. This is called *when-issued trading* and is usually referred to as *grey market*. Grey market trading does not take place for all the IPOs which come to the market – the sponsoring broker of the IPO firm would need to make an application to the LSE for this to be allowed. This application must be completed with sufficient time for approval and for a notification to be sent out via the LSE website.[54]

The LSE will only permit a grey market dealing in an IPO if it is satisfied that there will be a fair and orderly market in the trading of securities and that the trading of the IPO shares will be sufficiently liquid. Other criteria, such as that the security can be settled in electronic form and that there is sufficient demand for grey market trading, will also be applied by the LSE.

The LSE does not organise grey markets, rather it is the job of independent brokers who make forward markets in IPO shares on a when-issued basis. Examples of some independent brokers in the UK who may sometimes make when-issued forward markets in IPO shares are Spreadex (www.spreadex.com), City Index (www.cityindex.co.uk) and IG Index (www.IG.com). These brokers quote bid-ask spreads and investors can take a position (short or long) depending on their expectations.

Grey market prices are not only available from the broker but are also usually reported in the financial press. For example, during the road show period of Admiral Group's IPO, Reuters reported that Cantor Index was putting a grey market price of 245p–255p two days after listing. During the Moneysupermarket float, Cantor Index forecasted that the offer price for the company would be at the lower end of the 170p–210p price range (and they were right).

---

54   Since November 2007, LSE does not issue notices regarding grey market trading. Instead, information on grey market trading is disseminated through the Reference Data Service.

The demand for lastminute.com IPO shares was so large in the grey market that some analysts increased their valuations of the company by nearly £300m. In its IPO, Sabre Insurance started to trade on the grey market on 6 December 2017 with an offer price of 230p. In the opening trades, the price rose to 238p. By the close of the first day of grey market trading it stood at 257p.

Trading in the grey market usually begins on the day the IPO company publishes the offer price and notifies investors of the allocation of shares. The grey market trading ends a day before the stock begins to trade on the stock exchange (also known as the first day of unconditional dealing). According to LSE rules, grey market dealing normally lasts for a period of three business days. However, the exchange considers other trading periods, either shorter or longer than three business days, on a case-by-case basis.

The earliest settlement date for grey market trades is the first day of unconditional dealing but all trades conducted during the grey market only become binding if the IPO goes on to be officially listed on the LSE. IPO firms usually make this quite clear on the top page of their prospectuses. For example, Sabre's IPO prospectus carried the following warning:

> Conditional dealings in the ordinary shares are expected to commence at 8:00a.m. on 6 December 2017. It is expected that admission will become effective, and that unconditional dealings will commence at 8:00a.m. on 11 December 2017. All dealings in ordinary shares will be on a when-issued basis and of no effect if admission does not take place and will be at the sole risk of the parties concerned.[55]

Grey market trading is an interesting concept which has many benefits. It acts as a sort of pre-market for an IPO and helps in the process of price discovery when IPOs are officially admitted to the LSE. Grey market trading also provides valuable information to investors and should help them plan their trading strategy once the IPO is admitted to the stock exchange.

In a recent research paper, my co-authors and I did a long-term study of the UK's IPO grey market. We found that in the 1990s only 15% of the IPO firms chose to trade in the grey market. This increased to almost 80% in the last decade. Given that more and more UK IPOs are choosing to trade in this market, we were particularly interested in answering three important research questions. First, what types of firms choose to trade in the grey market? Second, does the decision to do so have any impact on the setting of the offer price? Third, what are the benefits of trading in the grey market?

---

55   Sabre Insurance Group Plc IPO prospectus.

We found that firms that are large and those that have higher future growth opportunities are more likely to choose to trade in the grey market. These firms appoint high quality underwriters and insiders sell a smaller proportion of their shares in the IPO. In other words, good quality IPO firms choose grey market trading. Interestingly the decision to trade in the grey market leads to a higher offer price compared with what it would have been had these firms chosen not to trade on the grey market. Grey market IPOs have higher trading volumes and exhibit better price accuracy.[56]

56   A. Khurshed, D. Kostas, A. Mohamed and B. Saadouni, 'Initial Public Offerings in the UK When-issued Market,' *Journal of Corporate Finance* 49 (2018), pp. 1–14.

4

The Performance and Survival of IPOs

In this chapter I discuss some interesting anomalies associated with IPOs such as short-run underpricing and long-run underperformance. Academics around the world have devoted a lot of effort to documenting and explaining reasons for such anomalies. I summarise some of the important explanations for such anomalies.

In the second part of the chapter I focus on the survival of IPO firms. This is one area which is quite under-researched, but it is of immense importance when looking at IPOs. The final section of the chapter provides an analysis of the performance of UK privatisation IPOs.

4.1 How IPOs perform when trading in their shares commences

We now shift our focus to some interesting facts about the share price performance of IPOs once they start to trade on the stock exchange. Imagine that you bought some shares in a recent IPO. If you paid £1 per share (this is the offer price), you may find that on the first day the shares start to trade, the share price of the company jumps to £1.20. If you choose to sell at this price, it would mean that for every share you own, you make a profit of 20p, i.e. a 20% return on your investment.[57] Given that your investment is for a couple of weeks (the time period when you applied for shares and the first day of trading), a 15% or 20% return is quite high.

---

57   This excludes the transaction costs such as the broker's fee.

Underpriced IPOs

It is common for IPOs on stock markets all around the world to show a jump in their share price on the first day of trading. This phenomenon is usually termed as *underpricing* or *leaving money on the table*. In 2008, when Visa conducted its IPO, it priced it shares at $44. At the close of the first day of trading, Visa's share price stood at $56.50, a gain of 28%. By the end of the first week of trading, Visa's shares were trading at $63.96, thus showing an underpricing of around 45%.

Visa's price run did not end here. By the end of the first month of trading, Visa's share price stood close to $70. Figure 4.1 charts the share price performance of the Visa IPO in its first month of trading.

Figure 4.1 – Short-run underpricing of Visa IPO

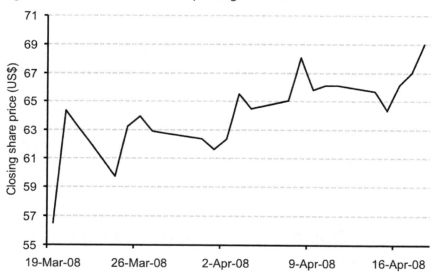

Sometimes the jump in the share price is not as high. In December 2017, the UK insurer Sabre Insurance Group Plc conducted its IPO on LSE pricing its shares at 230p. At the close of the first day of unconditional trading (Sabre chose to trade in the grey market), Sabre's share price stood at 250p, a gain of 9%.

Overpriced IPOs

There are occasions when the share price of an IPO drops on the first day of trading. This phenomenon is referred to as *overpricing*. Occasionally overpriced IPOs do come to the market but they are not as common as underpriced IPOs. Overpriced IPOs usually happen during stock market downturns.

Promethean World Plc, which conducted its IPO in March 2010 and priced its shares at 200p, saw its share price drop to 198p at the close of the first day of trading. Having said that, on the first day of trading Promethean World Plc opened at 210p and rose to a high of 211p before falling to 198p at the close of trading. All investors who sold their shares early on the first day of trading would still have made a profit on their investment. Similarly Ocado Plc, whose offer price was 180p, started trading at 159p. At the close of the first day of trading, the share price stood at 164p. Figure 4.2 charts the share price performance of the Ocado IPO in the first month of trading.

Figure 4.2 – Short-run overpricing of Ocado IPO

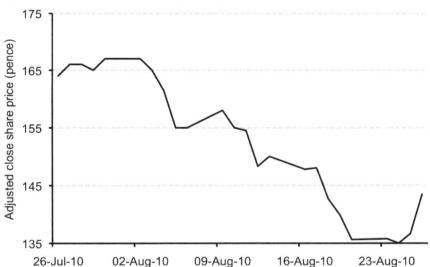

Overpriced IPOs were relatively common during the financial crisis of 2007–09 and even beyond. For example, in the first half of 2010, more than half of the European IPOs traded below their offer prices. Institutional investors were of the view that companies were being sold at unrealistic valuations. On 30 August 2010, the *Financial Times* ran the following story as its headline news:

Investors' anger rises at poor IPO returns

Institutional investors complain that investment bankers are siding too closely with corporate clients on IPOs, advising companies to price shares at levels that are too high.

However, the second half of 2010 saw most UK IPOs showing the traditional levels of underpricing again. Ever since, most IPOs have displayed underpricing albeit at a lower level than seen before the financial crisis.

A short and long-term perspective on IPO share price performance

The share price performance of IPOs can be studied both from a short-term and a long-term perspective. Short-term performance of an IPO usually refers to its share price performance on the first day of trading, the first week of trading, or at the most the first month of trading. Long-term performance usually refers to the share price performance in the first three years of the IPO and beyond.

Understanding how IPO share prices behave in the aftermarket is important for all parties. For investors who buy shares at the time of the IPO (at the time of the offer) or in the secondary market, the return on investment is tied to the share price performance of their firms. When share prices go up, the returns on investments go up as well.

From the point of view of the firms themselves, the competence of the directors/ managers of IPO companies is partially judged by the share price performance of their companies. Also, regulators are always keen to attract good quality firms to stock exchanges and so they also keep a close eye on the performance of companies after their IPO.

Short-term performance of IPOs

Studies of almost every stock market in the world have shown that on the first day of trading, on average, IPOs trade at a price which is higher than the offer price. As mentioned, this is termed underpricing. Academic research shows that the amount of underpricing varies from country to country. In the mid-1980s to early 1990s, French IPOs exhibited an average underpricing of 4.2%, while Malaysian IPOs were underpriced by nearly 80%. In the same period, IPOs in the US and in the UK showed underpricing levels of around 15%.[58]

During the dot-com bubble period, the level of underpricing in the US rose phenomenally to around 80%, though such a high increase in underpricing was not seen in UK IPOs during the same period. After the dot-com bubble burst in

---

[58] David Chambers and Elroy Dimson provide a comprehensive review of underpricing of UK IPOs since the first world war. They show that from 1917 to 1945 underpricing was around 3.8% compared with 9.15% in the period 1946 to 1986. Since 1986 (the year of Big Bang on the London Stock Exchange) underpricing has been even higher at 19%. The authors argue that underpricing in UK IPOs has been increasing over the last 100 years because of deterioration in the level of trust between investors, issuing firms and sponsors. Chambers and Dimson (2009).

2000, the IPO activity in Europe and the US was quite subdued. It only started to pick up in 2003–04 and continued to do so until the onset of the sub-prime crisis in 2007, which lead to great upheavals in the stock markets around the world. Indeed, one of the biggest causalities of the 2007–09 financial crisis was the US and European IPO market (except for AIM), which saw almost no IPO activity in these years.

Table 4.1 provides information on the average level of underpricing, before and during the financial crisis, in some important stock markets around the world.

Table 4.1 – IPO underpricing in major world stock markets (pre and during the financial crisis of 2007–09)

	IPOs in the years 2004–07		IPOs in the year 2008	
	Underpricing (%)	Number of IPOs	Underpricing (%)	Number of IPOs
LSE – Official List	16.5	90	−5.5	3
LSE – AIM	14.5	936	13.7	30
NYSE	15.3	85	6.1	10
NASDAQ	13.5	230	4.4	21
Deutsche Börse	14.9	137	10.6	4
Euronext	14.2	225	9.6	17
OMX	38.3	139	−2.9	13
Toronto Stock Exchange	16.1	129	N/A	18
Hong Kong Stock Exchange	27.9	96	−11.5	24

Source: Academic EurIPO Fact Book 2009.

As can be seen from Table 4.1, between 2004 and 2007, IPOs in some important European and US markets were underpriced by about 15%, which is similar to the historical levels of underpricing in these markets. However, as the financial crisis escalated in 2008, the level of IPO activity and also the level of underpricing in these markets showed a sizeable drop.

For example, in the year 2008 there were only three IPOs on the UK Main Market (Official List)[59] and on average these IPOs were overpriced by nearly

---

[59] This number excludes IPOs on the International Main Market and IPOs of financial firms.

6%. Similarly, on AIM, there were only 30 IPOs, though the average level of underpricing was a respectable 14%. The US markets also showed a drop in the number of IPOs and also the level of underpricing. Other markets such as the Deutsche Börse, Euronext, and OMX also showed lower IPO activity and a drop in the level of underpricing. The Hong Kong Stock Exchange not only saw a fall in the number of IPOs, it also showed a high level of overpricing.

Short-run performance of UK IPOs following the financial crisis (2009 and 2010)

The years 2009 and 2010 were quite challenging for the UK IPO market. Table 4.2 provides an analysis of the first trading day returns of all the IPOs that took place on the UK Main Market in 2009 and 2010. Table 4.3 does the same for the AIM. Table 4.2 excludes IPOs on the International Main Market and both Tables 4.2 and 4.3 exclude IPOs of financial firms.

The level of first day underpricing has been measured as:

$$\frac{\text{closing price on first day} - \text{offer price}}{\text{offer price}}$$

IPOs on the Main Market

The UK Main Market had only one non-financial sector IPO during 2009. This was of Exillon Energy, an independent oil producer with operations located in two oil-rich regions in northern Russia. The company placed 40.5m shares at 153p per share. Media reports covering the Exillon IPO mentioned that most of the shares on offer were bought by investors specialising in the oil and gas sector.

The company started to trade on the LSE on 17 December 2009 with an opening price of 150p. Over the next week Exillon's share price exhibited an interesting pattern. During the first day of trading the shares reached a high of 165p and a low of 150p, closing at 150p. Measuring the first day underpricing as the difference of the closing price and the offer price, the Exillon IPO was overpriced by nearly 2%. However, on the second day of trading the share price jumped to 198p, showing Exillon to be underpriced by nearly 29%.

Over the next three trading days Exillon's share price fell and at the close of trading on 24 December it stood at 160p. When trading resumed after Christmas, Exillon's share price shot up to 190p. Figure 4.3 charts the share price performance of the Exillon IPO since the time of its listing. Given that Exillon came with an IPO when most of the other firms either cancelled or postponed theirs, it did incredibly well in the first 15 months of its listing. This could partly be because of surging oil prices since the middle of 2010.

Table 4.2 – Underpricing of UK Main Market IPOs
during 2009–10

Name of IPO firm	Date of IPO	Offer price	On the first day of trading				Level of underpricing (%)
			Opening	High	Low	Close	
Exillon Energy	17 Dec 2009	153p	150p	165p	150p	150p	−2%
African Barrick Gold	24 Mar 2010	575p	605p	609p	580p	585p	2%
Promethean World	17 Mar 2010	200p	198p	198p	191p	193p	−4%
Super Group	24 Mar 2010	500p	502p	540p	499p	540p	8%
Essar Energy	7 May 2010	420p	394p	394p	358.5p	383p	−9%
Ocado Group	26 July 2010	180p	159.25p	164p	159.25p	164p	−9%
Betfair Group Plc	27 Oct 2010	1300p	1540p	1540p	1500p	1511.26p	16%
Flybe Group Plc	15 Dec 2010	295p	342p	342p	336.75p	337.25p	14%
Shaft Sink Holdings	23 Dec 2010	124p	133.75p	133.75p	133.75p	133.75p	8%

Figure 4.3 – Share price performance of Exillon IPO

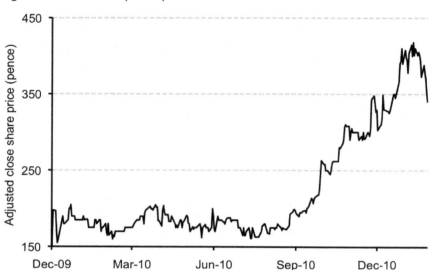

In the first half of 2010, only four IPOs took place on the LSE Main Market. Surprisingly, three of them came to the market on the same day, 24 March 2010.[60] African Barrick Gold, the largest gold producer in Tanzania, used a global offer to sell 101.08m shares at the price of 575p per share. By the close of the first day of trading, its shares were trading at 585p, showing a modest underpricing of 1.74%. Promethean World, a UK-based educational whiteboard maker, placed 92.9m shares at the price of 200p per share. The company traded at 193p at the close of the first day of trading, thus leading to an overpricing of 3.5%.

SuperGroup Plc, the fashion retailer, used a placing and an open offer to sell 25m shares at the price of 500p per share. Media reports at the time of the IPO suggest that both the institutional and retail tranches of the IPO were oversubscribed. This was despite of the fact that, out of the net £120m raised in the IPO, only £15m was to be used for the company's expansion while the remaining £105m was going to the company's owners and management. SuperGroup's opening price was 502p. The intraday high was 540p and the shares closed at 540p, thus showing an underpricing of 8%.

The chief executive of SuperGroup, Julian Dunkerton, said the company's successful flotation in jittery markets happened because the company is debt-free,

---

60 Promethean World's prospectus mentions 17 March 2010 as the first day of listing, whereas LSE documents show that the company started to trade unconditionally on 24 March 2010. The prices mentioned in the table relate to 17 March 2010.

is not private equity-backed and has a model investors could easily understand.[61] Unlike Exillon, SuperGroup did not show large price swings in the aftermarket. Apart from a brief period in May and December 2010, SuperGroup's share price has been on the way up since its listing. By early February 2011, SuperGroup was trading at a price which was nearly 2.5 times its offer price. This was an incredible performance by a fashion clothing firm in times of weak economic growth and low high street spending. Figure 4.4 charts the share price performance of the SuperGroup IPO in the months after its listing.

Figure 4.4 – Share price performance of SuperGroup IPO

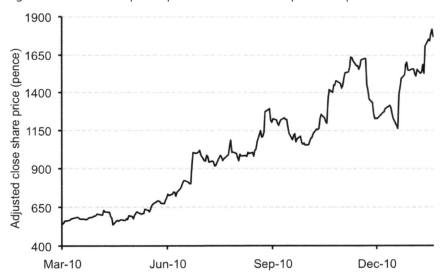

Another company with an IPO in the first half of 2010 was Essar Energy. Essar was admitted to the LSE on 7 May 2010 and offered shares only to institutional investors at a price of 420p per share. At the close of the first day of trading, its shares were priced at 383p, nearly 9% lower than the offer price.

In the second half of 2010 there were four IPOs on the LSE Main Market. Of the four, Ocado Plc's was the most widely covered by the financial press. Even though the IPO was sponsored by some of the top investment banks, investors (especially retail) showed very little interest in the company. By the close of the first day of unconditional trading, Ocado shares were trading almost 9% below their offer price.

---

61   Reported in Dow Jones Newswires, 12 March 2010.

Betfair conducted its IPO in October 2010. Though the IPO was made up entirely of secondary shares it was oversubscribed after the first day of book building. At the close of the first day of unconditional trading, the shares were trading nearly 16% above the offer price.

After shelving its flotation plans several times, Flybe, the first airline IPO in the UK for many years, successfully listed on the LSE in December 2010. Media reports at the time suggest that the IPO was almost two times oversubscribed at the offer price of 295p. At the close of the first day of unconditional trading, Flybe's shares were trading nearly 14% above their offer price. The last IPO of 2010 was that of Shaft Sink Holdings, a South African developer of shafts for underground mines. The IPO was underpriced by nearly 8%.

To summarise, after a gap of nearly two years, IPO activity returned to LSE's Main Market in 2010. While most of the IPOs in the first half of the year were overpriced, underpricing returned in the IPO market in the second half of 2010.

IPOs on AIM

During 2009 and 2010 AIM was more successful than the Main Market in attracting IPO business. Excluding the financial firms, there were four IPOs in 2009 and 39 IPOs in 2010.

Table 4.3 – Underpricing of UK AIM IPOs during 2009–10

Name of IPO firm	Date of IPO	Offer price	On the first day of trading				Level of underpricing
			Opening	High	Low	Close	
Indian Energy	2 Sept 2009	80p	82.50p	87p	84p	85p	6%
M Winkworth	12 Nov 2009	80p	83p	84p	84p	84p	5%
Avia Health Informatics	16 Nov 2009	60p	69.5p	73.88p	72p	73.88p	23%
Asian Plantations	30 Nov 2009	75p	79.5p	79.5p	79.5p	79.5p	6%
Oxford Nutrascience Group	12 Feb 2010	1.75p	2.00p	2.25p	2.00p	2.00p	14%
Kea Petroleum	15 Feb 2010	8p	9.25p	9.5p	8.0p	9.15p	14%
Equatorial Palm Oil	26 Feb 2010	17.5p	18.50p	17.00p	14.40p	15.00p	-14%

Name of IPO firm	Date of IPO	Offer price	On the first day of trading				Level of underpricing
			Opening	High	Low	Close	
Digital Barriers	4 Mar 2010	100p	114.5p	128p	117p	128p	28%
CSF Group	22 Mar 2010	55p	63p	63p	61p	61.75p	12%
EMIS Group	29 Mar 2010	300p	320p	330p	320p	328p	9%
EasyDate	30 June 2010	60p	64p	67p	64p	66.80p	11%
DP Poland	28 July 2010	50p	55.5p	57.5p	53.5p	54p	8%
iEnergizer	14 Sept 2010	116p	122.5p	142p	125p	138p	19%
Central Asia Metals	30 Sept 2010	96p	104.5p	104.5p	95p	99p	3%
Caparo Energy	12 Oct 2010	115p	115.25p	117.5p	114.5p	117.5p	2%
HaloSource	18 Oct 2010	135p	147.5p	165p	135p	163p	21%
Hangar8	10 Nov 2010	150p	160p	160p	155p	158p	5%
Zanaga Iron Ore	18 Nov 2010	156p	167p	167p	157p	163p	4%
Madagascar Oil	29 Nov 2010	95p	98p	98p	92.5p	92.72p	-2%
InternetQ	10 Dec 2010	120p	130p	145p	128p	143p	19%
Copper Development	13 Dec 2010	35p	41p	42p	36p	37.85p	8%
Ferrum Crescent	15 Dec 2010	10p	11.75p	12p	11p	10.75p	8%
Noricum Gold	17 Dec 2010	4p	5p	6.5p	5.37p	6p	50%

The level of first day underpricing has been measured as:

$$\frac{\text{closing price on first trading day} - \text{offer price}}{\text{offer price}}$$

In 2009, the first IPO on AIM was that of Indian Energy, a long-term owner and operator of wind farms in India, which came to the market on 2 September. The shares were priced at 80p. The opening price was 82.5p and the closing price was 85p, with an intraday high of 87p. The Indian Energy IPO thus showed a moderate underpricing of 6.25%.

M Winkworth, a UK-based franchised estate agency, offered 556,250 shares to institutional and retail investors at the offer price of 80p. Even though the money raised in the IPO was barely enough to cover the costs of flotation, on the first day of trading the shares closed at 84p, thus showing an underpricing of 5%.

Avia Health Informatics was another small IPO on AIM. It used a placing to sell 1.98m shares, two-thirds of which were placed to institutional investors and the rest were bought by the company staff. While the shares were sold at the price of 60p per share, the closing price on the first day of trading was 73.88p. Those who sold their shares at this price (73.88p was also the first day high) would have received a gross return of around 23% on their investment. The last AIM IPO of 2009 was that of Asian Plantations, a Singapore incorporated palm oil plantations company. The company sold 7.04m shares to institutional investors. The first day underpricing was 6%.

The first AIM IPO of 2010 was on 12 February. Oxford Nutrascience Group, a UK-based consumer healthcare company, used a placing to sell 62.85m shares at a price of 1.75p per share. The shares were trading at 2p at the end of the first day of trading thus exhibiting an underpricing of 14.29%. Kea Petroleum, a gas explorer in New Zealand, joined the AIM on 15 February 2010 by placing 75m shares at a price of 8p per share. At the end of the first day of trading its shares were selling at 9.15p, thus exhibiting an underpricing of 14.38%.

Equatorial Palm Oil, a palm oil producer which operates in Liberia, priced its shares at 17.5p. At the close of the first day of trading the shares were at 15p, thus overpriced by nearly 14%. Since the company used a placing to list on AIM, retail investors would not have been affected by this overpricing unless they bought shares in the open market on the first day of trading.

Digital Barriers, CSF Group and EMIS Group conducted their IPOs in March 2010. Digital Barriers' IPO was underpriced by nearly 28% while CSF and EMIS showed modest underpricing of 12.27% and 9.33% respectively. EasyDate conducted its IPO in June 2010 and showed underpricing of nearly 11%. All these four companies used a placing and therefore targeted only institutional investors.

In the second half of 2010 more than ten IPOs listed on the AIM. HaloSource Inc, a clean water technology company focussed on emerging markets, placed its shares to institutional investors at 135p per share. By the close of first day trading, the company shares were trading at 163p thus showing an underpricing of nearly 20%. InternetQ Plc, an Athens-based technology business conducted its IPO in December 2010 and was also underpriced by around 20%. Noricum Gold saw its price jump by 50% on the first day of trading. Other IPOs exhibited modest levels of underpricing from 2% to around 10%. Madagascar Oil was the only IPO which traded at a price lower than its offer price on the first day of listing in the second half of 2010.

Between 2009 and 2010, AIM continued to draw IPO firms from around the world. The fact that it was able to do this against the backdrop of a serious economic crisis demonstrates its importance as a destination for young and growing firms around the world.

Short-run performance of UK IPOs after the financial crisis (2011–2018)

After the financial crisis, IPO activity on LSE slowly picked up. Between 2011 and the first quarter of 2018, AIM has attracted more IPOs than the Main Market. However, for both markets, the number of IPOs is much smaller than the levels seen before the financial crisis. Table 4.4 provides an analysis of the first trading day returns of all the IPOs that took place on the Main Market and AIM from 2011 till March 2018. IPOs from financial firms have been excluded from this table.

Table 4.4 – Underpricing of UK IPOs during 2011–18

Year	AIM – No of IPOs	Average first trading day returns	Main Market – No of IPOs	Average first trading day returns
2011	39	13.23	9	−2.83
2012	36	13.26	10	5.73
2013	50	19.44	13	9.79
2014	68	9.84	30	5.85
2015	24	8.63	24	9.48
2016	35	11.67	12	12.08
2017	42	11.51	19	7.99
2018 (till Mar)	5	9.77	1	−7.70

The table above shows that between 2011 and 2013, both the number of IPOs and the level of underpricing picked up on both the AIM and Main Markets. The level of underpricing was much higher on AIM when compared with the Main Market. Though 2014 was a hot year in terms of large numbers of IPOs, the level of underpricing fell by almost half. During 2016, the year of the Brexit referendum, AIM attracted a sizeable number of IPOs. However the Main Market saw a sharp fall in the number of listings. During 2017 and the first quarter of 2018, the level of underpricing on AIM has remained stable; whereas activity on the Main Market was muted at the start of 2018, but picked up in the latter half of the year.

Why IPOs are underpriced[62]

The overwhelming evidence from almost all the markets of the world suggests that the short-run underpricing anomaly is not time and stock market specific. At the very basic level, two possible explanations can be offered for these abnormal returns:

1. IPOs are deliberately underpriced by underwriters.

2. Underwriters systematically fail to price IPOs correctly.

Most commonly it is assumed that the first of these possibilities, rather than the second, is at play.

Over the last three decades, academics have provided a number of theories to explain underpricing of IPOs. While some of these theories have been challenged and criticised, others have stood their ground. Below I give an academic survey of research that has been conducted into IPO underpricing and the explanations that this research has produced. The following explanations of IPO underpricing are covered:

1. Underwriter risk aversion hypothesis

2. Signalling the quality of the firm

3. Information asymmetry and the winner's curse hypothesis

4. Insurance hypothesis

5. Marketing

6. Ownership, control and agency costs hypotheses

---

[62] This section is largely based on my PhD thesis 'Initial Public Offerings: An Analysis of the Listing Contracts and the Post-IPO Performance of the UK Firms', University of Reading, 1999.

1. Underwriter risk aversion hypothesis

Initially, IPO underpricing was explained on the basis of risk aversion by underwriters. This is known as the *underwriter risk aversion hypothesis* and its basis is that "underwriters underprice new issues because of the uncertainty involved with the true value of the shares and to ensure a successful issue, or an offering that is quickly sold, is possibly over-subscribed, and enjoys some increase in price soon after the offering. This results in satisfied customers for the underwriter as well as satisfied corporate stockholders."[63]

However, there are suggestions that this explanation is not satisfactory because for it to be true, new issues distributed with a *best efforts*[64] contract should be more correctly priced than those distributed through a *firm commitment*[65] contract.[66] This is because the underwriter's risk is minimal for a best efforts contract. To add weight to the criticism of the underwriter risk aversion hypothesis, empirical evidence which casts doubt upon it has been produced.[67] Using a sample of 649 US IPOs during the period 1975–82, it was found that the underpricing for best efforts IPOs was much more severe than for firm commitment IPOs. The underpricing for best efforts was reported to be around 38%, which was about two times that of firm commitment offers (around 20%).

I also found similar results for UK IPOs. For a sample of IPOs which came to the Main Market during the years 1989–96, I found that placings (which are usually not underwritten) were more underpriced than public offers. The average level of underpricing in placings was around 11%, whereas the average level of underpricing in public offers was nearly 9%.[68] These results are inconsistent with the underwriter risk aversion hypothesis.

---

[63] F.K. Reilly, 'New Issues Revisited', *Financial Management* (Winter 1977), pp. 28–42.

[64] This is one of the methods by which US firms can conduct an IPO. In terms of risk-bearing, a best effort is equivalent to a UK placing.

[65] Firm commitment is another way in which US firms can conduct an IPO. In terms of risk-bearing, a firm commitment is equivalent to UK's public offer (offer for sale).

[66] S. Tinic, 'Anatomy of the IPOs of Common Stock', *Journal of Finance* 43 (1988), pp. 789–822.

[67] A.J. Chalk and J.W. Peavy, 'Initial Public Offerings: Daily Returns, Offering Types and the Price Effect', *Financial Analysts Journal* (1987), pp. 65–69.

[68] A. Khurshed and R. Mudambi, 'The Short-Run Price Performance of Investment Trust IPOs on the UK Main Market', *Applied Financial Economics* 12 (2002), pp. 697–706.

2. Signalling the quality of the firm

Another hypothesis put forward to explain underpricing posits that it is a deliberate attempt by the issuer to signal its quality to the market, to "leave a good taste in investors' mouths."[69] This is done so that when the firm returns to the market for a seasoned equity offering (SEO) it can fetch a higher price. It has been proposed that IPO firms pursue a multiple issue strategy when they choose the price and the percentage of equity offered – they work on the basis that a loss due to a low price at the IPO will be offset by a higher price at the subsequent SEO. Work has also been done to explain why IPO underpricing would result in a higher SEO price in terms of the information asymmetry between the issuers and the investors.[70]

It has been questioned whether firms do follow the two-stage selling strategy and whether the second stage of selling (SEO) provides any benefits at all. A counter-argument runs that the two-stage selling strategy is not applicable to markets like Germany and the UK, where shareholders benefit from pre-emptive rights to the SEO. In such cases there would be no benefit from signalling because the pricing of a rights issue is wealth neutral. In essence, the thinking is that the multiple issue strategy model, "which relies on high-value firms separating to receive more favourable terms in subsequent equity offers, cannot account for the observed underpricing in Germany, the United Kingdom, and any other country whose investors enjoy pre-emptive rights."[71]

Doubts have also been raised about the relevance of the underpricing signal. It has been questioned if, from a pool of signals, a firm would choose the underpricing signal, the other choices being hiring a quality underwriter, auditor or venture capital backer. It would be easier for the firm to make a decision if it is known that the underpricing signal is the most cost effective but it would be difficult to quantify the costs involved with all possible signals.[72]

Another variant of the signalling model posits that underpricing is the result of the issuers' desire to induce information production about their firm. It was argued that the issuers have information about the firm which investors do not. If the investors attempt to reduce this information asymmetry then this would impose a cost on them. The issuers of high quality firms are tempted to

[69] R. Ibbotson, 'Price Performance of Common Stock New Issues', *Journal of Financial Economics* 2 (1975), pp. 235–272.

[70] I. Welch, 'Seasoned Offerings, Imitation Costs and the Underpricing of IPOs', *Journal of Finance* 44 (1989), pp. 421–449; and I. Welch, 'Equity Offerings following the IPO: Theory and Evidence', *Journal of Corporate Finance* 2 (1996), pp. 227–259.

[71] T.J. Jenkinson and A.P. Ljungqvist, *Going Public: The Theory and Evidence on How Companies Raise Equity Finance* (Oxford University Press, 1996, 2001).

[72] Ibid.

maximise the investors' information so that this information will be reflected in the secondary market price of their firm's equity, increasing its expected value. To compensate the investors for their information gathering, the issuers underprice the IPO willingly. This model is similar to other signalling models in that it also assumes informational asymmetry and two-stage signalling but it does not view signalling as an effective device.[73]

3. Information asymmetry and the winner's curse hypothesis

The information asymmetry and winner's curse hypotheses are based on information asymmetry between the issuer and the underwriter, and also between the investors. Underpricing is justified as a natural outcome to compensate the party with more information (or less information in one of the models).

The information asymmetry hypothesis

Investment bankers possess a substantial information advantage over IPO issuers (typically small firms) and can use this to lower their own risk of loss. It has been suggested that underpricing results from such vertical information asymmetry and serves to compensate the underwriter for the use of his superior information.[74] A corollary of these arguments is that investment banks can use underpriced IPOs as a competitive instrument. That is, underpriced issues would only be allocated to favoured customers who regularly do business with the investment bank. This model assumes that underwriters (investment bankers) are better informed about the investor's demand than the issuers.

The investment banks also lend their prestige to the offering, thereby developing a better market than would exist otherwise. The issuer is also uncertain about the equilibrium price of its securities and hence lets the investment bank decide the issue price on its behalf. The model works on the assumption that the investment bank is more informed about the state of the capital market than the issuer. Since the more informed party needs to be compensated for its efforts to gather information, the issuer has to agree to underpricing by the investment bank. It was also shown that the level of discount was an increasing function of the issuer's uncertainty about the investor's demand.[75]

---

[73] T.J. Chemmanur, 'The Pricing of Initial Public Offerings: A Dynamic Model with Information Production', *Journal of Finance* 48 (1993), pp. 285–304.

[74] D.P. Baron, 'A Model of the Demand for Investment Banking Advice and Distribution Services for New Issues', *Journal of Finance* 37 (1982), pp. 955–976.

[75] Ibid.

This hypothesis was tested by examining the investment bank IPOs which were marketed by the banks themselves (i.e. self-marketed IPOs).[76] Commenting on the different possibilities of distribution of own securities, the possibilities were categorised as follows:

An issuer-underwriter can participate in the equity offering as:

(i) lead manager,

(ii) co-manager,

(iii) member of the distribution syndicate, or

(iv) selected leader.

It was pointed out that since the issuer and the underwriter are the same, the issue of information asymmetry does not arise. So according to the information-advantage model, one would expect those IPOs for which the issuer-underwriter does not act as the lead manager to be more underpriced. The IPOs of 38 investment banks that went public in the US in the period between 1970 and 1987 were examined (these were those IPOs where the banks also participated in the distribution of their own securities).

The results found that these IPOs were underpriced by about 7% on the first day of trading, thus contradicting the information advantage model. Moreover, for those IPOs where the issuer was also the lead manager, the underpricing was much more severe (13%). In contrast, for those IPOs were the issuer-underwriter was not the lead manager, the underpricing was only 2%. These conclusions show that the underpricing cannot be explained by vertical asymmetric information alone.

The winner's curse hypothesis

Of all the theories that make an attempt to explain underpricing, perhaps the best known is that based on the horizontal information asymmetry between investors.[77] While assuming that the issuer and the underwriter are completely uninformed about the true value of the shares on offer, the investors are classified into two groups:

1. Informed investors, who invest in information production and subscribe to IPOs only when they expect the aftermarket price to exceed the offering price.

2. Uninformed investors, who subscribe to every IPO indiscriminately.

---

[76] C. Muscarella and M. Vetsuypens, 'A Simple Test of Baron's Model of IPO Underpricing', *Journal of Financial Economics* 24 (1989), pp. 125–135.

[77] K. Rock, 'Why New Issues are Underpriced', *Journal of Financial Economics* 15 (1986), pp.187–212.

By assuming that the issuer and the underwriter have the same information, this model is free from the problem of conflicts of interest.

This hypothesis asserts that the uninformed investors face the winner's curse. Since the informed investors will not apply for overpriced issues, the uninformed investors will more than often end up being allocated the overpriced issues. After suffering repeated losses from the allocation of overpriced issues, the uninformed investors will leave the new issue market. It is assumed that the flight of the uninformed investors from the new issue market is bad news because the demand from the informed investors will not be enough to take up all the shares. So to entice and to keep the uninformed investors in the market, the firms willingly underprice their shares.

This is an optimal solution for both types of investors. The underpricing compensates the informed investors for their information production and the uninformed investors for the allocation bias. It is important to note that underpricing is not done because of rationing but because of the bias in rationing, the bias being that the expected allocation probability to the uninformed investors is smaller in good cases (where the issues are underpriced) than in bad cases (where the issues are overpriced).

The winner's curse model has been extended to show that the expected underpricing was an increasing function of the uncertainty of the price of the share in the market.[78] It was argued that there is an equilibrium relation between the expected underpricing of an IPO and the ex ante uncertainty about its value, and that the investment banks enforce this equilibrium. An investment bank is in a position to enforce the underpricing equilibrium because it is a repeated player in the IPO market.

So investment banks which do not follow the underpricing equilibrium by either underpricing too much or too little will be losers in the long-run. Empirical evidence for these propositions was presented by using a sample of 49 investment banks from 1977 to 1981 and examining the changes in their IPO market shares (i.e. changes in their share of the underwriting market) in the period 1981–82. It was concluded that those investment banks which deviated from the underpricing equilibrium by pricing either too low or too high experienced a reduction in their market shares in the subsequent market.

---

[78] R.P. Beatty and J.R. Ritter, 'Investment Banking, Reputation, and Underpricing of Initial Public Offerings', *Journal of Financial Economics* 15 (1986), pp. 213–32.

4. Insurance hypothesis

The insurance hypothesis suggests that IPO underpricing serves as a form of insurance against potential legal liabilities of issuers and their underwriters.[79] This hypothesis posits an implicit contract between issuers, underwriters and investors. Under this implicit contract, the investors are provided with excess returns as an insurance premium in return for which they are willing to overlook small errors (e.g. related to the disclosure requirements of securities regulations) without taking recourse to the courts. With reference to the US markets, it was suggested that the IPOs issued after the enactment of the Securities Act of 1933 should show more underpricing than those which were issued before 1933.[80] This hypothesis also predicts that the pricing of IPOs which are brought by issuers and investment banks whose exposure to legal liability is low, should be full.

The implications of the insurance hypothesis were tested with a data set of US IPOs that were issued before and after the Securities Act of 1933 and found that the Act had a significant effect on the pricing of new issues. The underpricing of a sample of 70 IPOs in the pre-SEC period was found to be around 5% compared with an underpricing of 11% in the post-SEC period. The study also did not find any relationship between the level of underpricing and underwriter reputation before 1933. In contrast, since 1933, the high reputation underwriters priced their IPOs more fully than the fringe underwriters. Lastly, the study found evidence that in the post-SEC regime, prestigious underwriters started avoiding highly speculative small IPOs. This market segmentation was absent in the pre-SEC period.

Empirical evidence has cast doubt over the insurance hypothesis. In 1983, a tough Securities Regulation Act (SRA) was passed in New Zealand (which has a similar legal environment to the US) but there was no change in underpricing in the pre- and post-SRA regime.[81] It was also found that underpricing does not reduce the probability of a lawsuit – evidence suggests that firms can be sued by investors of underpriced and overpriced shares alike and firms that are sued are no more or less underpriced than comparable firms that are not sued.[82]

---

[79] S. Tinic, 'Anatomy of the IPOs of Common Stock', *Journal of Finance* 43 (1988), pp. 789–822.

[80] The Federal Securities Act of 1933 specified considerably stricter criminal and civil liability provisions than those which existed before 1933.

[81] E.A. Vos and J. Cheung, 'New Zealand IPO Underpricing: The Reputation Factor', *Small Enterprise Research* 1 (1992), pp. 13–22.

[82] P.E. Drake and M.R. Vetsuypens, 'IPO Underpricing and Insurance Against Legal Liability', *Financial Management* 22 (1993), pp. 64–73.

Further criticism of the insurance hypothesis has been made on the basis that the hypothesis has oversimplified assumptions about the actual legal and financial liabilities for issuers and underwriters. The following observations were made:

1. Under the firm's liability policies, the major portion of any settlement is paid by the insurance companies, and underwriters (and the issuers) do not bear the cost of litigation and hence would have no incentive to insure themselves.

2. The Acts are about the irregularity in disclosure and not about the pricing so a finding of underpricing is immaterial to the outcome of the litigation.

This suggests that underpricing cannot be explained by the insurance hypothesis.

Evidence from a number of countries including Australia,[83] the UK[84] and Switzerland[85] shows that the risk of a legal suit is not economically significant.

5. Marketing

The marketing theory has its basis in the marketing problem that is faced by a firm that is being listed on the stock exchange for the first time. This problem is solved by using an underwriter. To gauge the investors' demand, the underwriters conduct the so-called road show to market an issue to investors prior to the public offer. These indications of interest from investors help the underwriters to price the issues.

By analysing the underwriter's marketing process it has been shown how the information it yields is used in pricing and allocating an IPO, with the conclusion that underwriters can reduce IPO underpricing by using their access to investors to collect information.[86] A contrary conclusion has also been reached, suggesting that the privileged access of underwriters to information increases underpricing.[87]

---

[83] P.J. Lee, S.L. Taylor and T.S. Walter, 'Australian IPO Pricing in the Short and Long-Run', University of Sydney Mimeograph, 1994.

[84] T.J. Jenkinson, 'Initial Public Offerings in the United Kingdom, the United States and Japan', *Journal of the Japanese and International Economies* 4 (1990), pp. 428–449.

[85] R.M. Kunz and R. Aggarwal, 'Why Initial Public Offerings are Underpriced: Evidence from Switzerland', *Journal of Banking and Finance* 18 (1994), pp. 705–724.

[86] L.M. Benveniste and P.A. Spindt, 'How Investment Banks Determine the Offer Price and Allocation of New Issues', *Journal of Financial Economics* 24 (1989), pp. 343–361.

[87] D.P. Baron and B. Holmström, 'The Investment Banking Contract for New Issues Under Asymmetric Information: Delegation and the Incentive Problem', *Journal of Finance* 35 (1980), pp. 1,115–1,138.

The model that suggests underwriters can reduce IPO underpricing projects underwriters as institutions that improve the efficiency of the IPO market. It was reasoned that underwriters face a problem when they wish to collect information useful to the pricing of an issue, namely that the investors have no incentive to reveal truthful information before the stock is sold. Thus, underwriters underprice the issue to compensate the investors for revealing positive information about the value of the stock. The underwriters can also use leverage of expected future profits to reduce underpricing.

In this model, the pre-market is seen as an auction conducted by the underwriter. This auction provides an opportunity for investors to understand how their indications of interest affect the offer price and the share allotments. The investors face a trade-off with respect to their revelations. If they do not reveal correct information then they can hope for immediate profits in the initial market but then this incorrect information will jeopardise the probability and quantity of shares being allocated to them.

The empirical implications derived from the marketing model are that underpricing is directly related to the ex ante value of investors' information, that the investment banks give priority to their selected customers and that underpricing is directly related to the level of interest in the pre-market. An important testable implication from the model is the relationship between the initial price range and the final offer price.[88] According to the model, an issue for which there is positive information revealed will be priced very near to the upper limit of the price range or even beyond the range. Some underpricing still needs to be included though, in order to compensate the investors for their truthful revelation. This has been called the partial adjustment phenomenon, according to which the underwriters do not increase the offer price to reflect the full information but they do it partially, thus allowing the investors to gain underpricing returns.[89]

Evidence has also been found in support of the proposition that IPOs whose final price is closer to the initial price ceiling should be more underpriced than those in the lower part of the range.[90] It was found that, on average, initial

---

[88] Amongst the other details filed at the time of the IPO's registration statement, is the initial high and low price range for the offering. These high and low prices represent the underwriter's "bonafide estimate of the final offer price" (Hanley 1993, p. 233).

[89] R. Ibbotson, J. Sindelar and J. Ritter, 'Initial Public Offerings', *Journal of Applied Corporate Finance* 1 (1988), pp. 37–45.

[90] K.W. Hanley, 'The Underpricing of Initial Public Offerings and the Partial Adjustment Phenomenon', *Journal of Financial Economics* 37 (1993), pp. 231–250; and C.B. Barry and J.R. Ritter, 'Initial Public Offerings and the Fraud on the Market', TCU and University of Florida unpublished manuscript, 1997.

returns are highest for IPOs that have an offer price greater than the upper end of the price range and lowest for those priced below the lower end of the price range. In cases where the pre-IPO information from the investors indicates a high demand for the issue, the amount of underpricing depends upon the negotiating powers of the issuer and the underwriter.[91] High reputation underwriters enjoy greater bargaining power than low reputation underwriters and hence they underprice issues to a greater extent.

6. Ownership, control and agency costs hypotheses

The issue of agency conflict[92] between the managers and the owners of a firm has also been addressed in the context of the underpricing of IPOs.[93] The existence of agency conflict is more likely in large firms that float SEOs to raise capital than in small firms which go public for the first time. This is because large firms are expected to have a wider separation between the management and the owners.

A model has been developed to show how underpricing is used by insiders to retain control over the firm.[94] Data on 69 UK IPOs for the period between 1986 and 1989 was used to show that underpricing is used to insure over-subscription of the issue. Once the issue is over-subscribed, the shares allocation can be rationed, which allows the owners to discriminate between investors and allocate shares to small-size share applications in order to avoid the concentration of shares in the hands of a few large investors or institutions.

With share-holdings distributed amongst many small investors, the likelihood of investor monitoring of managers becomes small because "in a corporation with many small owners, it may not pay any one of them to monitor the performance of the management".[95] A sub-sample of 13 firms for which detailed data on individual applications were available was used to confirm that the size

---

91   J.W. Cooney, A.K. Singh, R.B. Carter and F.H. Dark, 'The IPO Partial-Adjustment Phenomenon and Underwriter Reputation', Kansas State University working paper, 1999.

92   Agency conflict is a conflict of interest between people with different interests in the same assets. A classic example of agency conflict is the conflict between shareholders and managers of companies.

93   M. Jensen and W. Meckling, 'Theory of the Firm: Managerial Behaviour, Agency Costs and Ownership Structure', *Journal of Financial Economics* 3 (1976), pp. 306–360.

94   M.J. Brennan and J. Franks, 'Underpricing, Ownership and Control in Initial Public Offerings of Equity Securities in the UK', *Journal of Financial Economics* 45 (1997), pp. 391–413.

95   A. Shleifer, A. and R. Vishny, 'Large Stakeholders and Corporate Control', *Journal of Political Economy* 94 (1986), pp. 461–488. Quote from p. 461.

of the underpricing is negatively related to the size of large blocks assembled after the IPO.[96]

A further model has been presented that is in total conflict with this suggestion that underpricing is used by insiders to retain control of the firm. Instead, it is argued that the value of a firm is enhanced if the management allocates shares to large outside investors who are in a position to monitor the management. On the basis of this, a two-stage offering mechanism has been proposed in which the investment bank acts in the best interest of the issuer and allocates the shares to institutional investors in order to capture the benefits associated with better monitoring by institutions.[97]

Some recent developments in theories of underpricing

A recent set of research papers on IPO underpricing has come up with a totally different perspective on short-run underpricing and has the potential to turn understanding of IPO underpricing on its head.

One study examined how US IPOs are priced at the time of listing relative to their fair value.[98] The authors computed fair values for the IPO firms by using price multiples of non-IPO peer firms and then compared these fair values with the offer prices of the IPOs. They found that, relative to the peer firms, IPOs are systematically overvalued at the offer price. This overvaluation could be up to about 50%. The authors asserted that, while valuing IPOs, investors may be focussing too much on optimistic earnings growth forecasts and too little on profitability.

Another perspective on IPO overpricing has been offered that suggests,[99] along with the US study just mentioned, that relative to their intrinsic value, IPO shares are actually overpriced. It was argued that positive returns to investors on the first day of trading are not a result of issuers underpricing shares but are an outcome of the demand from over-optimistic sentiment traders.[100]

---

96 M.J. Brennan and J. Franks, 'Underpricing, Ownership and Control in Initial Public Offerings of Equity Securities in the UK', *Journal of Financial Economics* 45 (1997), pp. 391–413.

97 N.M. Stoughton and J. Zechner, 'IPO Mechanisms, Monitoring and Ownership Structure', *Journal of Financial Economics* 49 (1998), pp. 45–77.

98 A. Purnanandam and B. Swaminathan, 'Are IPOs Really Underpriced?', *Review of Financial Studies* 17 (2004), pp. 811–848.

99 F. Derrien, 'IPO Pricing in Hot Market Conditions: Who Leaves Money on the Table?', *Journal of Finance* 60 (2005), pp. 487–521; and A. Ljungqvist, V. Nanda and R. Singh, 'Hot markets, Investor Sentiment, and IPO Pricing', *Journal of Business* 79 (2006), pp. 1667–1702.

100 Sentiment traders, who are also referred to as noise traders, are usually retail investors.

These sentiment traders have a reservation price which is above the (already overpriced) offer price.

In a recent paper, my co-authors and I used the setting of the Indian IPO market to test the sentiment-based models of IPO initial returns. Though we didn't find overpricing in Indian IPOs, we did find evidence that suggests that information extraction plays a small role in driving IPO initial returns. It's the unmet demand of non-institutional investors that really drives the IPO share price upwards. We conclude that our results support the sentiment-based models of underpricing.[101]

Though the view that IPOs are overpriced is shared by only a few researchers, it has the potential to develop into a sizeable strand of IPO literature which could challenge the historic notion that IPOs are usually underpriced. I am hopeful that future research, both from developed and emerging markets, will shed further light on these new perspectives on short-run underpricing of IPOs.

Long-term performance of IPOs

An interesting characteristic of IPOs is that, relative to other quoted companies, investors on average lose out by holding shares of IPO companies in the long run. This underperformance sometimes lasts up to five years after the IPO. Evidence shows that, relative to other quoted companies, some IPO firms can underperform by 10% to 50% in the first three years after the IPO.

In Chapter 1, I discussed the IPO of Moneysupermarket in July 2007. Investors who bought shares in Moneysupermarket at the time of the offer (170p per share) and held on to their investments would have seen the share price of the company plummet to around 80p by the end of December 2010. Figure 4.5 shows how Moneysupermarket was consistently outperformed by the FTSE All-Share index from the end of 2007 onwards. Moneysupermarket paid a per share dividend of 1.63p in 2007, 3.5p in 2008 and 13.34p in 2009, so the overall return on investment would be better than the one that can be inferred from the graph.

---

[101] J. Clarke, A. Khurshed, A. Pande and A. Singh, 'Sentiment Traders & IPO Initial Returns: The Indian Evidence', *Journal of Corporate Finance* 37 (2016), pp. 24–37.

Figure 4.5 – Moneysupermarket's long-run share price performance v the FTSE All-Share index (rebased to 100)

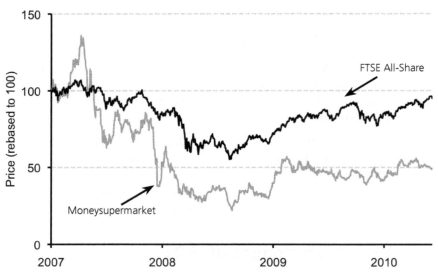

However, not all IPOs show long-run underperformance. Visa Inc outperformed the Dow Jones Industrial Average Index right from the beginning. Figure 4.6 depicts Visa's long-run share price performance during the first three years after the IPO.

Long-run underperformance of US IPOs

Large sample studies of the long-run performance of US IPOs find that, on average, they do not turn out to be good long-term investments. Jay Ritter, Cordell Professor of Finance at the University of Florida, is an expert on studies of IPOs. His website (site.warrington.ufl.edu/ritter/ipo-data/) has a lot of information relating to the underpricing, long-run performance, role and fee of underwriters, amongst other interesting IPO facts. Table 4.5 presents a part of the long-run performance table of US IPOs that Professor Ritter has compiled for his website.

Figure 4.6 – Visa's long-run share price performance v the DJIA (rebased to 100)

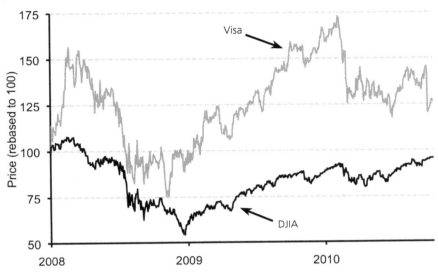

Table 4.5 – Long-run performance of US IPOs

Year	Number of IPOs	Average first day return	Average three-year buy and hold return	
			Raw return	Market adjusted
1980–89	2,043	7%	23%	−23%
1990–94	1,720	11%	46%	−6%
1995–98	1,893	18%	34%	−34%
1999–2000	858	65%	-53%	−32%
2001–15	1,661	14%	17%	−2%
1980–2015	8,175	18%	21%	−19%

Source: site.warrington.ufl.edu/ritter/ipo-data

Table 4.5 shows that over the last 35 years, US IPOs have underperformed the market by nearly 19% over the first three years of listing. The last two columns of the table show the average three-year buy and hold returns, raw and market adjusted, respectively.

Buy and hold return refers to the investment strategy where investors buy IPO shares, say at the time of offer or on the first day of trading, and hold on to these shares for a long period of time, three years in this case.

Raw return refers to the capital gains made from IPO investments and includes dividends. In other words, raw returns measure the return on your investment if you bought shares in IPO firms at the time of offer or on the first day of trading and sold them three years later.

Market *adjusted buy and hold returns* use a broad market index as a benchmark when measuring long-run returns. In this case, a CRSP (Center for Research in Security Prices) value-weighted index of Amex, NASDAQ and NYSE firms is used to measure the market adjusted returns. Market adjusted returns are a better measure of the long-run returns of IPOs.

Long-run underperformance of UK IPOs

Long-run underperformance has also been persistent for UK IPOs. In one of the first studies of UK IPO long-run performance, it was found that for the IPOs that came to the market in the 1980s, the three-year underperformance was between 8% to 23% depending on the benchmark used.[102] Other research showed that from the mid-1980s to the mid-1990s, a one pound investment in a UK IPO was worth less than 85 pence three years later.[103]

In one of my own papers, my co-authors and I have confirmed the earlier results of long-run underperformance and also studied the relationship between the pre-IPO financial performance of the firm (information on this is given in the IPO prospectus) and its subsequent post-IPO performance.[104] Further, we examined the relationship between managerial decisions taken before the IPO and the post-IPO performance of the firms. Three interesting results were found:

1. The more profitable a UK company is before the IPO, the worse is its post-IPO long-run performance.

2. The larger the size of the firm, the better is its long-run performance.

---

[102] M. Levis, 'The Long-Run Performance of Initial Public Offerings: The UK Experience 1980–1988', *Financial Management* 22 (1993), pp. 28–41.
[103] S. Espenlaub, A. Gregory and I. Tonks, 'Re-assessing the long-term underperformance of UK initial public offerings', *European Financial Management* 6 (2000), pp. 319–342.
[104] M. Goergen, A. Khurshed and R. Mudambi, 'The long-run performance of UK IPOs: Can it be predicted?', *Managerial Finance* 33 (2007), pp. 401–419.

3. The higher the stake sold by the insiders at the time of the IPO, the worse is the post-IPO performance.

Some of the previous studies on the long-run performance of UK IPOs are presented in Table 4.6.

Table 4.6 – Previous studies on the long-run performance of UK IPOs

Study	Period	Sample size	Long-run performance
Levis (1993)	1980–88	712	−8% to −23%
Espenlaub et al (2000a)	1992–95	249	−5.9% (VC-backed IPOs) −10.4% (unbacked IPOs)
Espenlaub et al (2000b)	1985–95	588	−15%
Goergen et al (2007)	1991–95	240	−13% to −22%
Hoque and Lasfer	1999–2006	830	−18.3%

Long-run performance of IPOs has been studied for a large number of stock markets around the world. For a detailed survey see *Going Public* by Jenkinson and Ljungqvist.[105] Since almost all the markets around the world show long-run IPO underperformance, it is important to know why this happens.

As with short-run underpricing, a number of theories have been suggested over a period of time to explain long-run underperformance of IPOs. I provide a summary of these below.

Theories of long-run underperformance of IPOs

Theoretical explanations for the long-run underperformance of IPOs are less abundant than those looking at short-run underperformance. The explanations put forward can mainly be placed into three groups:

1. Behavioural and expectations-based explanations.

2. The agency costs hypothesis.

3. Underperformance posited as a mis-measurement.

---

[105] T.J. Jenkinson and A.P. Ljungqvist, *Going Public: The Theory and Evidence on How Companies Raise Equity Finance* (Oxford University Press, 1996, 2001).

1. Behavioural and expectations-based explanations

This first group identifies the existence of underperformance and provides behavioural and expectations-based explanations for the phenomenon. A sub-group within this group tries to explain long-run underperformance using underpricing models. A number of hypotheses have been put forward and have been extensively tested.

A hypothesis that companies priced at the upper end of the initial price range perform better than those priced at the lower end was tested, but no support was found for it.[106] It has also been proposed that underperformance is due to the failure to include the value of legal damages in performance evaluation,[107] but a further study pointed out that the risk of litigation in not significant in most developed countries.[108]

Some researchers have put forward the *price support hypothesis* for explaining long-run underperformance. This hypothesis is based on the assumption that underwriters keep initial trading prices artificially high and once the price support has been withdrawn the prices will adjust downwards to their true market value.[109] A study was undertaken following this approach to test the implications of the hypothesis – the evidence found was partly inconclusive.[110]

It has also been suggested that share prices are set by the marginal, most optimistic investor.[111] As information flows increase with time, the divergence of expectations decreases and thus the prices are adjusted downwards, i.e. long-run performance is negatively related to the extent of divergence of opinion. It is difficult to test this hypothesis because it is difficult to measure the divergence of opinion.

Further studies have argued that firms go public when investors are over-optimistic about the growth prospects of IPO companies.[112] This means that

---

[106] H.K. Weiss, 'The Underpricing of Initial Public Offerings and Partial Adjustment Phenomenon', *Journal of Financial Economics* 34 (1993), pp. 231–250.

[107] P.J. Hughes and A.V. Thakor, 'Litigation Risk, Intermediation and the Underpricing of Initial Public Offerings', *Review of Financial Studies* 5 (1992), pp. 709–742.

[108] J.C. Alexander, 'The Lawsuit Avoidance Theory of Why Initial Public Offerings are Underpriced', *UCLA Law Review* 17 (1993), pp. 17–73.

[109] J.S. Rudd, 'Underwriter Price Support and the IPO Underpricing Puzzle', *Journal of Financial Economics* 34 (1993), pp. 135–151.

[110] A.P. Ljungqvist, 'IPO Long-Run Performance: Fact or Fiction?', Oxford University School of Management Studies Mimeograph, 1996.

[111] E.M. Miller, 'Risk, Uncertainty and Divergence of Opinion', *Journal of Finance* 32 (1977), pp. 1151–1168.

[112] J.R. Ritter, 'The Long-Run Performance of Initial Public Offerings', *Journal of Finance* 46 (1991), pp. 3–27; and R. Rajan and H. Servaes, 'Analyst following of Initial Public Offerings', *Journal of Finance* 52 (1997), pp. 507–529.

investors overpay initially but mark prices down as more information becomes available and so expected long-run returns decrease with the decrease in investor sentiment.

2. The agency costs hypothesis

The relation between long-run performance and ownership has been investigated as part of research on the agency costs hypothesis.[113] Using data from the US market, contrasting results have been found. One study – by Mikkelson et al. – found that, in general, the long-run performance both within one year of offering and during the first ten years of public trading is unrelated to ownership structure. However, Jain and Kini found a significant positive relation between post-IPO operating performance and equity retention by the original shareholders.

3. Underperformance as a mis-measurement

The third group of explanations for underperformance posits that it is a mis-measurement and it appears either because risk is not properly controlled for, or due to the problems related to the measurement of returns over long horizons. Underperformance could also be caused by the wrong choice of benchmark. The risk mis-measurement hypothesis proposes that the long-run underperformance may be due to a failure to adjust returns for time-varying systematic risk. No empirical evidence has been found for this hypothesis – a series of studies tried to adjust for risk but still found that newly-listed firms underperform.[114]

The literature on the problems related to the measurement of returns over long horizons is not recent – it has been argued over a period of time in various studies that several aspects of the long-run event study methodology create serious statistical difficulties.[115] Statistical inference conducted using traditional

---

[113] B.A. Jain and O. Kini, 'The Post Issue Operating Performance of IPO firms', *Journal of Finance* 49 (1994), pp. 1699–1726; and W.H. Mikkelson, M.M. Partch and K. Shah, 'Ownership and Operating Performance of Companies that Go Public', *Journal of Financial Economics* 44 (1997), pp. 281–307.

[114] J.R. Ritter, 'The Long-Run Performance of Initial Public Offerings', *Journal of Finance* 46 (1991), pp. 3–27; M. Keloharju, 'The Winner's Curse, Legal Liability and the Long-Run Performance of Initial Public Offerings in Finland', *Journal of Financial Economics* 34 (1993), pp. 251–277; and A.P. Ljungqvist, 'The Timing, Pricing and Long-Term Performance of Initial Public Offerings', Nuffield College, Oxford University, Ph.D. thesis (1995).

[115] E.S. Sefcik and R. Thompson, 'An Approach to Statistical Inference in Cross-Sectional Models with Security Abnormal Returns as Dependent Variable', *Journal of Accounting Research* 24:2 (1986); A. Brav, 'Inference in Long-Horizon Event Studies: A Parametric Bootstrap Approach', Seminar Paper presented at The Institute of Finance

testing methods, such as t-tests, are mis-specified because of potentially important violations of the underlying statistical assumptions.

It has been demonstrated that the measurement of the long-run performance of IPOs is sensitive to the benchmark employed.[116] So the possibility remains that imperfect benchmarking lies behind the poor long-run returns.

My discussion of the theories that explain short-run underpricing and long-run underperformance of IPOs is somewhat cursory. For those who would like to know more about these anomalies, I would once again recommend *Going Public*.[117] This book synthesises the vast amount of academic literature that has been produced on IPOs over a long period of time.

4.2 The survival of IPOs

It is important to focus not just on the short and long-run performance of IPOs but also on the survival of these firms. Survival refers to continued listing of IPO firms on the stock exchange[118] – a vital consideration since investors do not want to end up owning shares of IPO companies that are liquidated or delisted[119] from the stock exchange.

There have been a few large sample studies of the survival of IPOs. Most of these studies have looked at the survival of US IPOs and have covered a period from the mid-1970s to 2005. The failure rates have ranged from 2% to 9% in

and Accounting, London Business School (January 1997); B.M. Barber and J.D. Lyon, 'Detecting Long-Run Abnormal Stock Returns: The Empirical Power and Specification of Test Statistics', *Journal of Financial Economics* 43 (1997), pp. 341–372; and S.P. Kothari and J.B. Warner, 'Measuring Long-Horizon Security Price Performance', *Journal of Financial Economics* 43 (1997), pp. 301–309.

116 E. Dimson and P. Marsh, 'Event Study Methodologies and the Size Effect-The Case of UK Press Recommendations', *Journal of Financial Economics* 17 (1986), pp. 113–142; J.R. Ritter, 'The Long-Run Performance of Initial Public Offerings', *Journal of Finance* 46 (1991), pp. 3–27; A. Gregory, J. Matatko, I. Tonks and R. Purkis, 'UK Directors' Trading: The Impact of Dealings in Smaller Firms', *Economic Journal* 104 (1994), pp. 37–53; and E.F. Fama and K.R. French, 'Multifactor Explanations of Asset Pricing Anomalies', *Journal of Finance* 50 (1996), pp. 131–155.

117 Jenkinson and Ljungqvist, *Going Public*.

118 In fact it is an extremely important question for all the parties involved: the owners, managers and the regulators.

119 Delistings are not always bad news. If a firm is taken over by another, the shareholders of the target firm usually find that the share price of their firm goes up because of the takeover thus providing them handsome profits.

the first year of the IPO, 6% to 42% in the first two years of the IPO and 9% to 47% in the first five years after the IPO. A long period study of Canadian IPOs between 1986 and 2003 shows that on average nearly 20% of the IPOs fail in the first five years after their listing.[120]

A number of these studies looked at the relationship between IPO firm characteristics and their probability of survival in the post-IPO period. One study showed that older and larger firms survive for a longer period.[121] Similarly, firms with a high level of underpricing and a higher level of insider ownership also survive for longer periods.

Another study found that firms that exhibit good pre-IPO operating performance survive for a longer period[122] and that IPOs which are underwritten by top quality underwriters also survive for longer periods.

It has also been examined whether the presence of a venture capitalist affects the survival chances of an IPO and it was found that VC-backed IPOs survive for a longer period of time than those firms which are not backed by VC.[123] It was also found that IPOs with reputational auditors survive for a longer period of time.[124]

One interesting paper examined the survival of US IPOs over a period of ten years after their listing.[125] The study covered the US market from 1973 to 1991. It was found that the characteristics (such as profitability and growth rates) of companies conducting an IPO significantly changed over the period of the study. It was also found that firms that came for an IPO during the later part of their sample period showed lower profitability and higher growth. These changes in IPO firm characteristics are associated with a sharp decline in survival rates of IPOs. It was argued that the cost of equity has declined over a period of time, thus allowing younger and less profitable firms to conduct an IPO.

---

120 C. Carpentier and J. Suret, 'The Survival and Success of Canadian Penny Stock IPOs', *Small Business Economics* 36 (2011), pp. 101–121.

121 D. Hensler, R. Rutherford and T. Springer, 'The Survival of Initial Public Offerings in the Aftermarket', *Journal of Financial Research* (1997), pp. 93–110.

122 B.A. Jain and O. Kini, 'The life cycle of initial public offerings', *Journal of Business Finance & Accounting* 26 (1999), pp. 1281–1307.

123 B.A. Jain and O. Kini, 'Does the presence of venture capitalists improve the survival profile of IPO firms?', *Journal of Business Finance & Accounting* 27 (2000), pp. 1139–1176.

124 B.A. Jain and C. Martin, 'The association between audit quality and post-IPO performance: A survival analysis approach', *Review of Accounting and Finance* 4 (2005), pp. 50–75.

125 E.F. Fama and K.R. French, 'New lists: Fundamentals and Survival Rates', *Journal of Financial Economics* 73 (2004), pp. 229–269.

The survival of IPOs on AIM

In a 2012 paper, my co-authors and I studied the survival of IPOs on the London Stock Exchange's AIM market.[126] To the best of my knowledge this is the first paper on IPO survival which studies the UK IPOs. The idea came about as a result of skirmishes in the long, drawn-out and bitter battle between the US and UK stock markets (and their regulators) over market share in new stock market listings. On 9 March 2007, the *Financial Times* ran the following story as its headline news:

> **Top SEC official calls AIM a casino: LSE hits back, hinting remarks sparked by jealousy**
>
> A spat between the London Stock Exchange [LSE] and the US Securities and Exchange Commission [SEC] loomed yesterday after Roel Campos, an SEC commissioner, described London's junior AIM market as a casino on which 30% of listings were 'gone within a year'.

The SEC quote came against the backdrop of large numbers of new listings, including those from a growing number of US companies, and those on AIM. The US position argued that AIM had captured its large market share in new listings due to its lax regulation at a time when US regulation had become more burdensome due to the Sarbanes-Oxley reforms. In its response to the SEC remark, the LSE categorically rejected the SEC claim arguing in turn that failure rates on AIM were a mere 3%, not 30% as claimed by the SEC. My co-authors and I set out to check which of the SEC or the LSE was correct.

We studied all the IPOs that came to AIM from its inception in 1995 through to the end of 2004. After excluding companies that entered AIM without conducting an IPO (such as through an introduction), we were left with a sample of nearly 900 IPOs, which were tracked until July 2009. We found that in the first year of the IPO, a total of 6% of the AIM firms were delisted. This figure is higher than what the LSE claimed (3%), but much lower than what the SEC alleged (30%).

When we broke down the failure rate of 6% according to the reasons for the failure, we found that 2% of the IPOs were delisted because of a merger or an acquisition (which is usually good news for the shareholders of the target firm), only 1% undergo a voluntary liquidation, 2% have their quotations suspended and the rest are delisted because of other reasons. In the second and third year after the IPO, the failure rate jumped up to 25% (cumulative for years one to three). Nearly half of these delisted firms underwent a merger or an acquisition.

---

[126] S. Espenlaub, A. Khurshed and A. Mohamed, 'IPO Survival in a Reputational Market', *Journal of Business Finance & Accounting* 39 (2012), pp. 427–463.

In the fourth and fifth years after the IPO, a further 30% of the AIM IPOs were delisted. Again the major reason for the delisting was a merger or an acquisition.

So, in total, in the period studied, nearly 55% of IPOs left AIM within five years of listing. This result has important implications for investors. Those who intend to be long-term investors in IPOs not only face the risk of underperformance, they also face an investment in firms, half of which would not survive beyond a five-year period. We will discuss the implications of such a result in the next chapter.

4.3 An analysis of the performance of UK privatisation IPOs

Over the last three decades, the UK has witnessed massive privatisation of state-owned enterprises (SOEs). From the sale of the state's shareholding in BP in 1977 to the privatisation of the National Air Traffic Services (NATS) in 2001, more than 50 SOEs have been privatised by various governments. The real push towards privatisation in the UK is often credited to the Thatcher government, during which period (and beyond), most SOEs were sold through offers for sale, thereby providing opportunity for retail investors to invest.

The attempt to include UK households in these IPOs was intentional. In the 1980s, individual holdings of UK ordinary shares were at an all-time low (they had dropped from 54% in 1963 to 28% in 1981).[127] The government at that time was keen to promote a shareholding democracy. It was also hoped that wider share ownership would bring liquidity to the stock market. As a result, tender offers were replaced by offers for sale and most of these had higher than usual discounts (i.e. higher underpricing).

It is interesting, then, to consider the short and long-run return for investors in these privatisation IPOs. Table 4.7 shows details of the first day returns on some of the main privatisation IPOs in the UK.

Some of these privatisations took place in tranches. For example, British Petroleum, British Telecom, British Aerospace, Cable & Wireless and a few others were sold in two or more rounds. The table only covers the sale of the first tranche.

---

127 *Financial Times*, 15 November 1983.

Table 4.7 – Short-run performance of UK privatisation IPOs

Company name	First trading day	Percentage of shares offered	Offer price (per share)	Price on the first trading day	Underpricing (%)
British Petroleum (BP)	10.06.77	49	845p	912p	8
British Aerospace Plc	20.02.81	52	150p	170p	13
Cable & Wireless Plc	06.11.81	49	168p	197p	17
Amersham International	25.02.82	100	142p	188p	32
Britoil Plc	23.11.82	51	215p	196p	−9
Associated British Port Holdings	16.02.83	52	112p	138p	23
Enterprise Oil	02.07.84	100	185p	185p	0
Jaguar	10.08.84	100	165p	179p	8
British Telecommunications	03.12.84	50	130p	172p	32
British Gas	08.12.86	97	135p	147.75p	9
British Airways	11.02.87	98	125p	169p	35
Rolls-Royce	20.05.87	97	170p	232p	36
British Airports Authority	28.07.87	96	245p	291p	19
British Steel	05.12.88	100	125p	127.25p	2
Anglian Water	12.12.89	98	240p	288.5p	20
Northumbrian Water	12.12.89	98	240p	297p	28
Severn Trent	12.12.89	98	240p	271p	13
Southern Water	12.12.89	98	240p	281p	17
Thames Water	12.12.89	97	240p	276p	15
Welsh Water	12.12.89	98	240p	281p	17
Wessex Water	12.12.89	98	240p	294p	23
Eastern Electricity	11.12.90	98	240p	288p	20
East Midland Electricity	11.12.90	98	240p	290.5p	21
London Electricity	11.12.90	98	240p	282p	18
Manweb	11.12.90	98	240p	306p	28
Midlands Electricity	11.12.90	98	240p	284p	18
Northern Electric	11.12.90	98	240p	282.5p	18

Company name	First trading day	Percentage of shares offered	Offer price (per share)	Price on the first trading day	Underpricing (%)
Norweb	11.12.90	98	240p	292p	22
Seeboard	11.12.90	98	240p	282p	18
Southern Electric	11.12.90	98	240p	290p	21
South Wales Electric	11.12.90	98	240p	304p	27
South Western Electric	11.12.90	98	240p	290p	21
Yorkshire Electric	11.12.90	98	240p	299.5p	25
National Power	12.03.91	61	175p	212.5p	21
Power Gen	12.03.91	60	175p	212p	21
Scottish Power	18.06.91	96	240p	255.5p	6
Northern Ireland Electricity	18.06.93	97	100p	126.5p	27
Railtrack	20.05.96	98	380p	409.5p	8
British Energy	15.07.96	88	198p	192p	−3
AEA Technology	26.09.96	100	280p	323.5p	16
Royal Mail	15.10.13	52	330p	489p	48

Source: Adapted from M. Florio and K. Manzoni, 'Abnormal returns of UK privatisations: from underpricing to outperformance', *Applied Economics* 36 (2004), pp. 119–136.

While a large majority of these privatisations took place through an offer for sale, tender offers were used for Britoil and Enterprise Oil. Interestingly, both these IPOs did not show any underpricing. For example, Enterprise Oil traded at its offer price on the first day of trading while the share price of Britoil was lower than its offer price on the first day of trading (the shares were overpriced by nearly 9%).

In comparison, the average level of underpricing in all the other privatisations was nearly 18%. As stated above, the British government chose to privatise these firms using offers for sale with higher than normal levels of underpricing because this fitted with one of the main aims of the privatisations – to increase UK household participation in the stock market. The most recent privatisation of Royal Mail resulted in the highest level of underpricing ever seen.

Now let's consider whether privatisation IPOs also exhibit long-run underperformance.

Evidence from various studies suggests that privatisation IPOs have overperformed. In one of the earliest studies of the long-run performance of UK privatised IPOs, it was found that they outperformed market benchmarks in the first three years after their listing. However, this outperformance was not exhibited by other IPOs.[128] In another study, which looked at the internal rate of return of investments in UK privatisation IPOs, it was found that at on average they provided a higher internal rate of return than the FTSE All-Share index.[129]

In 2004, the *Investors Chronicle* published data on the performance of the 28 major privatised companies that were still listed at the time. A £100 investment in Associated British Ports on the first day of trading (the IPO took place in February 1983) would have grown to £7,148.25 by March 2004 (with dividends reinvested). Similarly, £100 invested in British Petroleum would have grown to £5,155.48. However, not all the privatisations are success stories in the long run. By March 2004, a £100 investment in AEA technology (IPO in September 1996) was worth only £126.21, while the same investment in Corus was worth £91.24. The bottom of the league table was British Energy; a £100 investment in July 1996 was worth only £4.70 by March 2004. Royal Mail has performed exceptionally well since its IPO. A £100 investment in Royal Mail's IPO in October 2013 was worth £168 in April 2018.

So from the work of Levis, Cawthron and the *Investors Chronicle* study we can see that by and large, in the long run, privatisation IPOs outperform market benchmarks. This means that a long-term investment in privatisation IPOs is usually a profitable investment strategy. However, potential investors should still be careful when analysing such IPOs for their investment potential as not all the privatisation IPOs outperform in the long term.

---

[128] M. Levis, 'The Long-Run Performance of Initial Public Offerings: The UK Experience 1980–1988', *Financial Management* 22 (1993), pp. 28–41.
[129] I. Cawthron, 'Regulated Industries: Returns to Private Investors to May 1998', CRI, Occasional Paper 11, London (1999).

5

Investing in IPOs

When making an investment in an IPO, it is clearly important to choose well as not all IPOs perform in the same way in the short and long term. There are no fool-proof rules for IPO stock selection because no one knows for sure how an IPO firm will perform in the after-market. However, sometimes there are obvious signs which can help in making informed decisions on IPO investment.

In this chapter I discuss where information on firms planning IPOs can be found and how to analyse an IPO prospectus. Towards the end of the chapter I discuss some strategies for investing in IPOs. As with any investment strategy, these are just theories – they by no means guarantee successful investments.

5.1 Where to find information on firms planning an IPO

As mentioned, firms that plan to list on the stock exchange have to go through a formal process of application. The media (such as the *Financial Times,* Reuters and Bloomberg) usually run stories on some of the IPOs in the pipeline and the *Investors Chronicle* has a dedicated section with reviews of forthcoming IPOs. Specialist websites such as ALL IPO (www.allipo.com) and Hargreaves Lansdown (www.hl.co.uk) provide a table with a lot of information on forthcoming IPOs, primarily those which are coming to the AIM. Digital Look (www.digitallook.com) and Hargreaves Lansdown also provide key information on firms planning an IPO on the Main Market and AIM of the LSE.

5.2 The IPO prospectus

As discussed in Chapter 1, firms conducting an IPO in the UK have to publish an IPO prospectus under the Prospectus Rules of the FCA. The Prospectus Rules of the FCA provide directions on how firms should draw up their prospectuses. These directions include details on the general contents of the prospectus, its format and the minimum information to be included. The FCA rules clearly define the order of the main parts of the prospectus as:

- A clear and detailed table of contents.

- A summary.

- Risk factors linked to the company.

- Other items included in the schedules and building blocks according to which the prospectus is drawn up.

Issuing firms are then free to define the order in which to present the required information items included in the schedules and building blocks sections. The overriding goal is to provide the necessary information in non-technical language, to enable investors to make informed assessments of the firm. The prospectus is therefore the most valuable source of information on the firm planning an IPO. Though all participants of the IPO (the issuing firm, the sponsors, auditors, lawyers, etc.) are jointly liable for each other's actions, the directors of the issuing firm bear the ultimate responsibility for the veracity and accuracy of the IPO prospectus.

Over the years IPO prospectuses have grown in thickness as firms have tended to provide information about themselves which is over and above what is required to be disclosed in accordance with the FCA rules. In the prospectus, firms have to disclose key information on the IPO such as:

- The number of shares to be sold.

- The price per share.

- Percentage of shares to be sold.

- The underwriters.

- The financial accounts.

- The risk factors.

- A timetable for investors to apply for shares.

Detailed information is also required on the business of the firm, its directors and senior management.

Financial information (usually covering the last three years) forms a large part of the prospectus. The later sections of a prospectus usually contain information about the material contracts of the firm, lockup agreements and a breakdown of the ownership structure of the firm at the time of the IPO.

With so much information available in the prospectus it can be difficult to know what to make of the information that is presented and then to glean the relevant detail. I will spend some time now clarifying these points. I first start with a snapshot of the type of information that is usually provided in a prospectus. The topics discussed below are in no particular sequence.

As an example, I discuss the prospectus that was issued by Bakkavor Group Plc – it conducted its IPO on the LSE Main Market on 16 November 2017.

The front part of the prospectus

The front page

The first page of the prospectus starts with a set of declarations required by law, such as that the prospectus is being made available to the public as required by the Prospectus Rules and that the company and its directors accept responsibility for the information contained in the document. There is also information about the day when admission becomes effective. In the case of Bakkavor Group Plc, the prospectus declared that admission would become effective and that unconditional dealings in ordinary shares would commence on 16 November 2017. Some prospectuses even mention the time at which trading will commence. This is usually 8:00a.m. for London Stock Exchange IPOs.

Also provided on this page is information on the number of shares offered, the price per share, and the name of the sponsor and book runner. This is an important piece of information as it provides an idea of the size of the issue and who the sponsor is. Usually, top-quality sponsors bring good companies to the market.

The first page also carries other information such as the legal obligations of the sponsor and sometimes a rider that the prospectus does not form part of any offer or invitation to sell or issue securities other than the ordinary shares.

A contents list usually follows. This highlights the sections of the prospectus that relate to information on directors, the expected timetable relating to the offer, financial information and additional information on the issuing firm. For those who do not want to read through the full financial information, a summary of key facts is quite handy.

In the case of Bakkavor, page four of the prospectus contains a summary of disclosure requirements known as *elements*. These elements conform to the European Union's Prospectus Directive, have a common format and are usually ordered from Section A to Section E. Bakkavor's prospectus devotes almost ten pages to this information. Section A carries an introduction and warnings to potential investors. Section B provides IPO company details such as current operations and principal activities of the firm, current trends, current shareholders and historical financial information. Bakkavor's prospectus mentioned that the company is the leading provider of fresh prepared food in the UK and has a growing international presence in the US and China. It is the number one producer by market share in the UK in each of the four fresh prepared food product categories: meals, salads, desserts, and pizza and bread. As of 2016, Bakkavor had a manufacturing network of 25 factories and three distribution centres in the UK, three factories and one under construction in the US and eight factories and one under construction in China. Readers could also find information about the state of the fresh prepared food market and how it was expected to grow in the next few years. Bakkavor went on to describe its group structure and major shareholders. All this information helps to form a picture of the company and the market in which it operates.

Section C has information on the share issue, the rights attached to the shares on offer and the dividend policy of the company. Bakkavor mentioned that it planned to start paying dividends from 2018 and that the group was targeting a 40% payout ratio. This information is quite handy for investors planning a long-term investment in the company. Subsequent sections convey information on issues such as key risks specific to the company and its industry, net proceeds of the IPO, lockup agreements and how the money raised in the IPO will be used by the company. For potential investors, all this information contained in a summary form, is crucial in forming the first impression about the company.

Beyond the summary section, an IPO prospectus is divided into a number of parts. Usually Part 1 of the prospectus is dedicated to a detailed discussion of the risk factors the IPO company is facing or is likely to face in the future, and there is a forewarning to potential investors that they should consider all the risk factors before deciding to invest in the company. Bakkavor had 14 pages dedicated to the discussion of potential risk factors ranging from the adverse impact of Brexit and the company's dependence on a small number of clients without long-term contracts to the fluctuations in exchange rates. Such detailed discussion of the risk factors is common and should be considered in perspective. We discuss this piece of information later in the chapter.

The next part of the prospectus provides information on the directors, secretary, advisers and the head office details of the issuing firm. Expected timetable of principal events and offer statistics follow.

Expected timetable for the offer

The timetable published in Bakkavor's IPO prospectus is shown in Table 5.1.

Table 5.1 – Timetable from Bakkavor's IPO prospectus

Prospectus published	10 November 2017
Announcement of the offer price and allocation	10 November 2017
Admission and commencement of unconditional dealings in the shares on the London Stock Exchange	8am on 16 November 2017
Crediting of shares to CREST accounts	16 November 2017
Despatch of definitive share certificates (where applicable)	From 16 November 2017

Statistics relating to the IPO

This section acts as a good starting point for those who wish to get a grasp of the amount of money that will be raised in the IPO and the number of shares that will be sold. The summary table from Bakkavor's prospectus is shown in Table 5.2.

Table 5.2 – Summary table from Bakkavor's prospectus

Offer statistics[1]	
Offer price (per share)	180 pence
Number of shares in the offer	144,856,397
— New shares	55,555,555
— Existing shares	89,300,842
% of the issued ordinary share capital being offered in the offer	25.0%
Number of shares in issue following the offer	579,425,585
Market capitalisation of the company at the offer price	£1,043m
Estimated net proceeds of the offer receivable by the company[2]	£86m
Estimated net proceeds of the offer receivable by the selling shareholders[3]	£158m

Notes on Table 5.2:

(1) Assumes all the reorganisation steps set out in paragraph two of Part 14 (Additional Information) are completed in full. To the extent that these steps are not completed in full, the offer will not proceed and admission will not be sought.

(2) The estimated net proceeds receivable by the company are stated after deduction of the estimated underwriting commissions and other fees and expenses of the offer (including VAT) to be paid by the company, which are currently expected to be approximately £14m. The company will not receive any of the net proceeds from the sale of the existing shares in the offer by the selling shareholders.

(3) The estimated net proceeds receivable by the selling shareholders are stated after deduction of the estimated underwriting commissions payable by the selling shareholders, which are currently expected to be approximately £3m.

The next few sections of the prospectus are dedicated to a discussion of the business, the industry in which the company operates, information on the directors and senior managers and the corporate governance set-up of the company. Potential investors should read these thoroughly to form an opinion of management skills, the company's position in its industry and its corporate governance set-up. These are helpful in forming a long-term view of the company and what it stands for. Financial details, including historical financial information, form the next part of the prospectus.

Consolidated financial statements

The next section of the prospectus usually provides information on consolidated financial statements, which are an important source of information on the financial health of the company. For Bakkavor the combined and consolidated income statement showed that profits had steadily grown over the last three years. The firm had a profit of £12.8m in 2014, which grew to £51.3m in 2016, a four-fold increase.

A statement of financial position showed that the total assets of the firm remained stable over the last three years before the IPO (£1,240.4m in 2014 to £1,248.5m in 2016). Total liabilities had been decreasing over the same period. All this painted quite a healthy picture of the firm's finances.

When reading the consolidated financial statements, a few important points need to be borne in mind.

Indebtedness

First, care should be taken where an IPO firm shows that its indebtedness has significantly increased over the two or three years before the IPO. Highly indebted firms are risky and may end up choosing between growth and management of their debt – two issues which may not go hand in hand all the time. This is one of the reasons why VC-backed IPOs have not been in much demand over the last decade. The common perception is that VCs pile their firms with a large amount of debt before selling off their stakes at the time of the IPO.

Profit figures

If the profit figures look good, the source of high profits has to be deduced. Areas to think about include whether the firm operates in a niche area, whether it is expanding into other markets and whether it has a patent which protects it from competition. In the case of Bakkavor, the firm was operating in the fresh prepared food market which has been steadily growing. The company was rapidly making inroads in foreign markets and its customers included some of the most reputable and well-known grocery retailers. The increase in gross profits of Bakkavor could be attributed to increasing sales with the cost of goods sold somewhat fixed at around 72% to 73% and the profit margin steadily increasing over the previous three years.

Balance sheets

The combined and consolidated balance sheets also provide information on assets and liabilities. When looking at the balance sheet information, inventories are an important area. If inventories are growing faster than sales, it might mean that demand is falling. In the case of Bakkavor, between 2014 and 2016 inventories decreased by 8% while sales increased by 8%. This shows that the demand for Bakkavor's products was increasing over this period of time.

Cash flow statement

The cash flow statement provides an interesting insight into the cash flowing in and out of the company and is organised into three parts:

1. *Cash generated from operating activities* provides information on the future declines in sales and earnings by signalling when a company is having problems in selling its inventory or collecting cash it is owed. In the case of Bakkavor, cash generated from operating activities is shown to have increased from £86.4m in 2014 to £112.1m in 2016.

2. *Cash used in investing activities* gives information on whether the company is cutting back on capital expenditures, amongst other things.

3. *Cash from financing activities* reveals if the company has received a cash infusion from banks or shareholders.

A healthy company should generate excess cash from its operations and should show negative cash balances in its *cash used in investing activities* and *cash generated from financing activities*. This is because a self-sustaining business should be able to pay off its debt and should be able to finance new investments internally. In case of Bakkavor, this was the case over the entire three-year period before its IPO.

Other important parts of the prospectus

Corporate governance

A lot of attention is usually paid to the corporate governance set-up of the IPO company. The prospectus will specifically state if the company fully complies with the UK Corporate Governance Code[130] and if not what actions it will take to do so. In the case of Bakkavor, the company was in full compliance with the UK Corporate Governance Code. Page 71 of the prospectus states:

> The board is committed to the highest standards of corporate governance. Save as set out below, as of the date of this prospectus and on and following admission, the board will comply fully with the UK Corporate Governance Code (the "Governance Code") published in April 2016 by the Financial Reporting Council. As envisaged by the Governance Code, the board has established an audit committee, a nomination committee and a remuneration committee. If the need should arise, the board may set up additional committees as appropriate.

> The Governance Code recommends that at least half the board of directors of a UK-listed company, excluding the chairman, should comprise non-executive directors determined by the board to be independent in character and judgement and free from relationships or circumstances which may affect, or could appear to affect, the director's judgement.

> The board intends to achieve full compliance with the Governance Code, and intends to appoint one additional independent non-executive director within nine months of admission.

Details of the offer

In this section of the prospectus the issuing firm discusses the reason for its IPO and how it intends to use its IPO proceeds. In the case of Bakkavor, the total

---

[130] The UK Corporate Governance Code (formerly referred to as the Combined Code) sets out standards of good practice in terms of accountability and relations with shareholders, board structure and remuneration.

amount raised was predicted to be £86m, net of underwriting commissions and other estimated fees and expenses. The company intended to use the offer proceeds to reduce its current debt, as a further investment in the business and to provide a partial realisation of the investment in the group by certain existing shareholders. IPO proceeds were also to be used to pay fees and expenses related to the offer, which were estimated to total approximately $14m.

Most IPO firms use a part of the proceeds to retire their debts and use the remainder for growth. If almost all the money raised from the IPO is being used for retiring debt then there should be a sound explanation provided in the prospectus for such a decision by the firm.

Lockups

Lockups (or lock-in arrangements) are agreements between the existing shareholders of the IPO firm (such as managers, directors, venture capitalists and other individual and institutional investors) and the underwriter, whereby the existing shareholders agree not to sell their holdings (or a part of their holdings) for a specified length of time after the IPO. Bakkavor had the following lockup agreement in its listing prospectus:

> Pursuant to the underwriting agreement, the company has agreed that, subject to certain exceptions, during the period of 180 days from the date of admission, it will not, without the prior written consent of the joint global Co-ordinators and Peel Hunt, issue, offer, sell or contract to sell, or otherwise dispose of, directly or indirectly, or announce an offer of any shares (or any interest therein or in respect thereof) or enter into any transaction with the same economic effect as any of the foregoing.

> Pursuant to the underwriting agreement and related arrangements, the selling shareholders and the directors have agreed that, subject to certain exceptions, during the period of 180 days in respect of the selling shareholders, and 365 days in respect of the directors, in each case from the date of admission, they will not, without the prior written consent of the joint global co-ordinators and Peel Hunt, offer, sell or contract to sell, or otherwise dispose of, directly or indirectly, or announce an offer of any shares (or any interest therein in respect thereof) or enter into any transaction with the same economic effect as any of the foregoing.[131]

Lockup agreements can be interpreted as a signal of the insiders' commitment to work in the interests of the outside shareholders after the firm has conducted its IPO. Lockup agreements also help to reduce information asymmetry that arises in IPOs. The longer the insiders' shares are locked up for, the more time

---

131 Bakkavor's listing prospectus, p. 181.

new investors have to collect information about the newly listed firm. Lockups also ensure that insiders maintain a significant interest in the firm after the IPO. Though there are no regulations in the UK that require a minimum lockup period in IPO firms, almost every firm chooses to have a lockup.

When assessing a particular lockup, the key thing to check is who is locked up, for how long and if there are any escape clauses buried in a footnote. A lockup is not set in stone and there are instances where insiders sell their holdings (or a part of them) before the expiry of the lockup mentioned in the prospectus. My research has shown that there were a few cases where insiders of IPOs conducted on the Main Market sold a part of their holdings before lockup expiry.[132] These cases are quite rare though, and the research also showed that even on the day of lockup expiry it is usual for many directors not to sell their holdings. This means that on the whole lockups can be seen as credible signals of a company's commitment towards its new shareholders.

When looking at the interaction between the old shareholders (insiders) and the new shareholders (those who buy shares at the IPO), it is also appropriate to think about the number of shares insiders sell at the time of the IPO. This can act as another signal of the commitment of the insiders towards the new shareholders. As discussed in Chapter 1, companies conducting an IPO can sell both primary and secondary shares. Primary shares are created on behalf of the company as part of the IPO, while secondary shares are the existing shares which the original shareholders sell at the time of the IPO. The money raised by selling primary shares goes to the company accounts while the money raised by selling secondary shares goes to the shareholders who sell their stakes.

Most IPOs have a mix of primary and secondary shares. In the case of Bakkavor, the existing shareholders sold almost 89m shares at the time of the IPO. At the same time 55.5m newly issued shares were also issued. This is a common occurrence in IPOs. For Baakavor, it was evident from the sale of secondary shares that the existing shareholders were using the IPO to realise a part of their investment in the company. Table 5.3 provides information on the interests of the directors and senior managers of Bakkavor before and immediately following the admission.

---

132 S. Espenlaub, M. Goergen, A. Khurshed and M. Remenar, 'Do Directors Trade after IPO Lockup Expiry?', *Handbook of Research on IPOs* (Edward Elgar, 2013).

Table 5.3 – Bakkavor Plc: interests of directors and senior management

Name of director/ senior manager	Number of shares prior to admission	Percentage of issued share capital	Number of ordinary shares following admission	Percentage of enlarged issued share capital
Agust Gudmundsson	155,833,130	29.7	145,333,130	25.1
Lydur Gudmundsson	155,833,130	29.7	145,333,130	25.1
Todd Krasnow	–	–	–	–
Robert Q. Berlin	–	–	–	–
Simon Burke	–	–	–	–
Denis Hennequin	–	–	–	–
Peter Gates	–	–	–	–
Sue Clark	–	–	–	–
Pippa Greenslade	–	–	–	–
Mike Edwards	–	–	–	–
Einar Gustafsson	–	–	–	–
Ivan Clingan	–	–	–	–

An example of an IPO where fewer secondary shares were sold in comparison of the primary shares is provided by Promethean World. Table 5.4 shows what was offered in Promethean's IPO.[133]

Table 5.4 – Promethean World's IPO

Number of shares in the offer	92,874,117
— to be issued by the company	57,018,405
— to be sold by the selling shareholders	35,855,712

Nearly 39% of the shares sold in Promethean's IPO were secondary. This means that almost 60% of the total money raised (£111.4m of the total £185.7m raised in the IPO) in the Promethean IPO was going to the company.

---

[133] Promethean World's IPO prospectus, p. 27.

Table 5.5 provides details of Promethean's directors' and senior managements' shareholdings at the time of the IPO. These details have been adapted from Promethean's IPO prospectus. The last column of the table shows the percentage of insiders' shares (owned before the IPO) sold in the IPO.

Table 5.5 – Promethean World: Interests of directors and senior management

Director/Member of the senior management team	Number of shares with direct or indirect interest	Percentage of existing issued share capital	Number of shares immediately upon admission	Percentage of issued share capital on admission	Percentage of shares sold in the IPO
Graham Howe	11,041,162	8	11,041,162	6	0
Jean-Yves Charlier	6,820,223	5	5,591,514	3	18
Neil Johnson	793,588	0.6	595,192	0.3	25
Lord Puttnam	190,537	0.1	190,537	0.1	0
Tony Cann	89,125,288	62	79,287,412	40	11
Philip Rowley	95,268	0.1	132,768	0.1	39 (holdings increased)
Dante Roscini	95,268	0.1	120,268	0.1	26 (holdings increased)
Paul Pickup	1,088,155	0.8	630,864	0.3	42
Andy Dennis	388,697	0.3	293,429	0.1	25
Brent Taggart	388,696	0.3	293,428	0.1	25
Iwan Streichenberger	476,344	0.3	362,022	0.2	24
Reggy-Charles Degen	388,697	0.3	293,429	0.1	25
Mark Elliott	623,059	0.4	467,295	0.2	25
Eugene Viskovic	438,237	0.3	352,495	0.2	20
Paul Berry	571,611	0.4	457,290	0.2	20

Table 5.5 shows that while the majority of directors and senior management team of Promethean sold a part of their holdings in the IPO, there were a few who actually bought shares. Two non-executive directors bought shares in the IPO so as to maintain their 0.1% stake in the company. The chairman and the

senior independent director did not sell any shares in the IPO. This is a positive signal that the directors and senior management are committed to the company.

Risk factors

As discussed at the start of this chapter, in the part of the prospectus dedicated to risk factors, companies discuss how their business could be materially and adversely affected by a number of risks. This provides an insight into the risks relating to the business, the IPO and tax. The amount and extent of risk-related information provided in the prospectus may differ from one IPO to the other. For example, while Bakkavor devoted 14 pages of its prospectus to discussing various risks the company may face, Royal Mail's IPO prospectus had no less than 35 pages covering a discussion of various risks faced by the company.

Some of the risks mentioned in IPO prospectuses will be specific to the business of the company. For example, Bakkavor mentions that the company is dependent on a small number of clients. In comparison, Promethean mentions that it is subject to certain environmental regulations that, if breached, could result in substantial fines, product recalls or exposure to liability claims.

A large number of risks will be common between IPO firms. For example, both Bakkavor and Promethean mention risks relating to global economic conditions, the failure to recruit and retain key management staff, the actions of competitors, exchange rate fluctuations, and legal claims, amongst others.

Information relating to risks needs to be digested rationally. Some companies may be more forthcoming with a list of risks they foresee but this does not make them more liable to succumb to the risks than firms that do not discuss much about their potential risks. Most companies make a genuine effort to provide as much information as possible on potential risks the firm faces in their IPO prospectuses.

Terms and conditions of the offer

Depending on the IPO firm's decision to sell its shares to institutional investors or retail investors, or both, the IPO prospectus will carry the relevant terms and conditions of the offer. Listing prospectuses of IPOs in which shares are being offered only to institutional investors carry a section with details on who could apply for shares. For example, Flybe – which conducted its IPO in December 2010 – mentioned in its prospectus that the global offer was being made by way of an offer of ordinary shares to certain qualified investors, including to institutional investors in the UK, certain institutional investors outside the US and by private placements to qualified institutional buyers (QIBs) in the US.

The prospectus specifically mentioned that members of the ordinary public (retail investors) could not apply for shares.

IPOs with a retail tranche also provide a list of terms and conditions for retail investors. Non-compliance with these terms usually leads to the applications being rejected by the company. In the case of SuperGroup, one of the conditions of retail application was that it was made by a domestic (UK) investor, for a minimum of £250 in value and, if the investor was applying online, the application should not exceed £13,000. Another condition related to multiple applications not being permitted.

Details on refunds are also provided. If an application is unsuccessful or if a number of shares applied for could not be allocated, the balance of any monies is usually returned to the investor without interest. Once the investors have made their application, they cannot revoke or withdraw their application unless the admission fails to go ahead. However, in line with current UK listing rules, applicants now have the right to withdraw their applications if a supplementary prospectus is issued by the IPO firm. IPO prospectuses contain information on such withdrawal rights.

The Ocado IPO provides an example of one where a supplementary prospectus was issued. In its supplementary prospectus, Ocado introduced a new reduced price range (the original price range of 200p to 275p was reduced to 180p to 200p), which was a result of a weak investor demand. In the final pricing statement on 21 July (the first day of grey market trading), Ocado fixed the offer price at 180p. Those who had applied for shares in Ocado (their applications were based on the original price range of 200p to 275p) had until midnight on 22 July to withdraw their applications. If retail investors did withdraw their applications, the unsold shares were to be picked up by the underwriters to the issue.

Some IPOs attach special terms and conditions to the offer. For example, Ocado mentioned in its prospectus that all successful applicants would have to agree to hold their shares in the Ocado Share Account, a company-sponsored nominee arrangement providing a convenient way of holding ordinary shares. Other details such as warnings on money laundering, mode of payment for the shares and the basis of the allocation of shares are also provided.

It is interesting to note that companies usually retain discretion when allocating shares to investors. In the case of Bakkavor, the IPO prospectus mentioned that the basis of allocation for applications would be solely determined by the company and its selling shareholders in consultation with the joint global coordinators.

The middle part of the prospectus

The middle section of the IPO prospectus is customarily made up of two parts. The first usually contains detailed information on directors and senior management, and the corporate governance set-up of the firm. The second part provides in-depth financial information on the company. This information takes a lot of time to read but it is valuable.

At present, IPO prospectuses provide a lot of detail on the background of the company's directors and senior management. Readers should look for appropriate collective experience and expertise of the board and the management team. They should also pay attention to the board structure; such as whether there are any non-executive directors on the board and if there are any signs of conflicts of interest. A strong management team provides a credible signal about the quality of the firm. High-profile directors and successful managers are expected to continue working in the interests of the new shareholders.

Companies also discuss their corporate governance set-ups in a lot of detail. Even though compliance with the corporate governance requirements of the UK Corporate Governance Code is voluntary, the Prospectus Rules of the FCA ask for a statement explaining why the company does not comply with the UK Corporate Governance Code, if relevant. Important areas are the development of appropriate corporate governance structures such as the audit and remuneration committees, and their memberships. It should also be examined whether the role of the CEO and the chairman is split. For IPO firms where the CEO is also the chairman of the firm, too much power and reliance gets concentrated with a single individual, thus reducing security for investors.

As mentioned, the middle section of the prospectus also provides detailed financial information concerning the IPO firm's assets and liabilities, financial position, and profits and losses. The Prospectus Rules of the FCA require companies to provide audited historical financial information covering the latest three financial years and the audit report for each of these three years. Consistency in revenues and profits is important – erratic or declining financial performance usually signals that the firm is quite risky.

It should be remembered that not all companies will show profits before their IPO. IPOs from the IT and biotechnology sectors usually come to the market at the pre-profit stage. This is to allow them to raise money for the necessary R&D. Some companies provide profit forecasts in their IPO prospectuses. This is not required by regulation so, in principle, this should act as a positive signal about the firm's confidence in achieving targets.

The end part of the prospectus

The last few sections of the prospectus usually contain information on the tax consequences of holding shares (for example taxation on dividends and disposals) and a separate section on *additional information*.

Apart from the general information on incorporation and articles of association, the *additional information* section also contains details on the firm's dividend policy, voting rights, and information on directors and senior management not covered in the earlier parts of the prospectus. This will disclose the shareholdings of the directors and senior managers, and also if there are any substantial shareholders (apart from the board and management team) at the time of the IPO.

In case of SuperGroup, the prospectus mentioned that there were no substantial outside shareholders before the IPO. However, AXA Framlington, a specialist equity fund manager, bought 3.2m shares at the time of the IPO, thus owning 4% of the enlarged issued share capital. For those who are really keen to know more about the directors and senior managers of the IPO firm, a lot of information on service contracts and letters of appointment, remuneration and lockup contracts of the directors and senior managers can be found here.

The final pages of a listing prospectus usually contain a section on *material contracts*. These relate to the placing agreements, sponsor and broker agreements, loan agreements (if any), and any legal and arbitration proceedings, amongst others.

5.3 What else to look for in an IPO firm

A prospectus provides the most in-depth and reliable information about a firm planning an IPO. Signals of a good-quality firm include a sound track record, a sound corporate governance set-up and consistent financial performance in the years leading up to the IPO.

In addition to this, the firm should also display a viable and realistic business plan. Having read the prospectus, it is useful to step back and think about the information gathered from it. The financial performance of the company may have been quite consistent in the past, but the future business plan of the firm for how this performance can be maintained or further improved needs to be clearly laid out. The business plan, which is one of the building blocks for the IPO prospectus, should not be over-optimistic and must be backed up by credible projections of sales and costs. The company must have sufficient working capital to meet the projected requirements and should have a good source of future revenue.

Further thought might also be given to lockups, as not all of them carry the same importance. If the owner-director of the firm is locked up for longer than other directors then this is a good signal. Sometimes the company itself is locked up. For instance, Resolution Ltd, which conducted an IPO in December 2008, agreed to a three-year lockup for the shares it subscribed to in its placing.

The timing of the IPO and market sentiment are also important considerations. A top quality company coming for an IPO may end up with lower than expected market valuations and even a failure to float if the market conditions are difficult. This is what happened to a number of firms in the three years following the start of the financial crisis in 2007. Changes in the economic environment and shifts in market sentiment are beyond the control of any firm. Therefore, when evaluating an IPO firm, the market conditions at the time of the planned IPO should be assessed.

5.4 Ten summary rules for IPO investment

There are no guaranteed trading rules that can be used to profit from IPOs. However, past research into various aspects of IPOs allows us to generate a summary list of ten important points that can at least form the basis of an assessment of investment potential in an IPO. The ten rules below are based on evidence from previous IPOs and may not hold true under future conditions.

- **Rule 1**: To make a profit from an underpricing of shares in the IPO, shares should be bought at the offer price (at the time of the offer) and sold at the first available opportunity on the first day of trading. Prior research has shown that almost all underpricing is captured in the early trades on the listing day.

- **Rule 2**: Unless buying shares in a privatisation IPO, care is needed when making a long-term investment in IPOs:

  - Multinational firms usually do not underperform in the long run.

  - Highly underpriced IPOs usually underperform in the long run.

  - The more profitable a firm is (in the pre-IPO period), the worse is its long-run performance.

- **Rule 3**: VC-backed firms tend not to be in fashion in an uncertain economic climate. However, these IPOs tend to be of better quality so should not be ignored outright.

- **Rule 4**: IPOs where only secondary shares are being sold or where insiders are selling a majority of their stake at the time of the IPO should be avoided.

- **Rule 5**: More than 50% of AIM IPOs delist from the stock exchange within five years from listing.

- **Rule 6**: IPOs which are underwritten by top quality sponsors are usually of good quality. It should be borne in mind though that in an uncertain economic climate – such as that between 2007 and 2010 – even IPOs that are underwritten by top investment banks could be postponed or sold at a revised lower price.

- **Rule 7**: If the share price of an IPO is sticky in the aftermarket, it may be a sign of price stabilisation from the sponsor. When sponsors remove price stabilisation (usually within four weeks of listing) the share price is expected to fall. Selling towards the end of this 30-day period should be avoided as this is the time when price stabilisation usually ends.

- **Rule 8**: Selling shares around the lockup expiry period should be avoided as share prices usually drop at this time.

- **Rule 9**: AIM IPOs are usually more risky than those conducted on the Main Market.

- **Rule 10**: IPOs conducted on the International Main Market are those of non-UK firms. Extra time and effort has to be given to reading their prospectuses in great detail.

Bibliography

Alexander, J.C., 'The Lawsuit Avoidance Theory of Why Initial Public Offerings are Underpriced', *UCLA Law Review* 17 (1993), pp. 17–73.

Barber, B.M. and Lyon, J.D., 'Detecting Long-Run Abnormal Stock Returns: The Empirical Power and Specification of Test Statistics', *Journal of Financial Economics* 43 (1997), pp. 341–372.

Baron, D.P., 'A Model of the Demand for Investment Banking Advice and Distribution Services for New Issues', *Journal of Finance* 37 (1982), pp. 955–976.

Baron, D.P. and Holmström, B., 'The Investment Banking Contract for New Issues Under Asymmetric Information: Delegation and the Incentive Problem', *Journal of Finance* 35 (1980), pp. 1115–1138.

Barry, C.B. and Ritter, J.R., 'Initial Public Offerings and the Fraud on the Market', TCU and University of Florida unpublished manuscript, 1997.

Beatty, R.P. and Ritter, J.R., 'Investment Banking, Reputation, and Underpricing of Initial Public Offerings', *Journal of Financial Economics* 15 (1986), pp. 213–32.

Benveniste, L.M. and Spindt, P.A., 'How Investment Banks Determine the Offer Price and Allocation of New Issues', *Journal of Financial Economics* 24 (1989), pp. 343–361.

Brav, A., 'Inference in Long-Horizon Event Studies: A Parametric Bootstrap Approach', Seminar Paper presented at The Institute of Finance and Accounting, London Business School (January 1997).

Brennan, M.J. and Franks, J., 'Underpricing, ownership and control in initial public offerings of equity securities in the UK', *Journal of Financial Economics* 45 (1997), pp. 391–413.

Carpentier, C. and Suret, J., 'The Survival and Success of Canadian Penny Stock IPOs', *Small Business Economics*, 36 (2011), pp. 101–121.

Cawthron, I., 'Regulated Industries: Returns to Private Investors to May 1998', CRI, Occasional Paper 11, London (1999).

Chalk, A.J. and Peavy, J.W., 'Initial Public Offerings: Daily Returns, Offering Types and the Price Effect', *Financial Analysts Journal* (1987), pp. 65–69.

Chambers, D., 'Gentlemanly Capitalism Revisited: A Case Study of the Underpricing of Initial Public Offerings on the London Stock Exchange, 1946–86', *The Economic History Review* 62 (2009), pp. 31–56.

Chambers, D. and Dimson, E., 'IPO Underpricing over the Very Long Run', *Journal of Finance* 64 (2009), pp. 1407–1443.

Chemmanur, T.J., 'The Pricing of Initial Public Offerings: A Dynamic Model with Information Production', *Journal of Finance* 48 (1993), pp. 285–304.

Clarke, J., Khurshed, A., Pande, A. and Singh, A., 'Sentiment Traders & IPO Initial Returns: The Indian Evidence', *Journal of Corporate Finance* 37 (2016), pp. 24–37.

Cooney, J.W., Singh, A.K., Carter, R.B. and Dark, F.H., 'The IPO Partial-Adjustment Phenomenon and Underwriter Reputation', Kansas State University working paper, 1999.

Derrien, F., 'IPO Pricing in Hot Market Conditions: Who Leaves Money on the Table?', *Journal of Finance* 60 (2005), pp. 487–521.

Dimson, E. and Marsh, P., 'Event Study Methodologies and the Size Effect-The Case of UK Press Recommendations', *Journal of Financial Economics* 17 (1986), pp. 113–142.

Drake, P.E. and Vetsuypens, M.R., 'IPO Underpricing and Insurance Against Legal Liability', *Financial Management* 22 (1993), pp. 64–73.

Espenlaub, S., Garrett, I. and Mun, W.P., 'Conflicts of Interest and the Performance of Venture Capital-backed IPOs: A Preliminary Look at the UK', *Venture Capital* 1 (2000a), pp. 325–349.

Espenlaub, S., Gregory, A. and Tonks, I., 'Re-assessing the Long-term Underperformance of UK Initial Public Offerings', *European Financial Management* 6 (2000b), pp. 319–342.

Espenlaub, S., Goergen, M. and Khurshed, A. 'Lock-in Expiry and Directors' Trading Activity: An Empirical Investigation', Working paper, Manchester Business School 2008.

Espenlaub, S., Khurshed, A. and Mohamed, A., 'IPO Survival in a Reputational Market'. *Journal of Business Finance & Accounting* 39 (2012), pp. 427–463.

Espenlaub, S., Goergen, M., Khurshed, A. and Remenar, M., 'Do Directors Trade after IPO Lockup Expiry?', *Handbook of Research on IPOs* (Edward Elgar, 2013).

Fama, E.F. and French, K.R., 'Multifactor Explanations of Asset Pricing Anomalies', *Journal of Finance* 50 (1996), pp. 131–155.

Fama, E.F. and French, K.R., 'New lists: Fundamentals and Survival Rates', *Journal of Financial Economics* 73 (2004), pp. 229–269.

Florio, M. and Manzoni, K., 'Abnormal Returns of UK Privatisations: From Underpricing to Outperformance', *Applied Economics* 36 (2004), pp. 119–136.

Goergen, M., Khurshed, A. and Mudambi, R., 'The Strategy of Going Public: How UK Firms Choose Their Listing Contracts', *Journal of Business Finance & Accounting*, vol. 33(1–2), pp. 79–101 (2006).

Goergen, M., Khurshed, A. and Mudambi, R., 'The Long-run Performance of UK IPOs: Can it be Predicted?', *Managerial Finance* 33 (2007), pp. 401–419.

Gregory, A., Matatko, J., Tonks, I. and Purkis, R., 'UK Directors' Trading: The Impact of Dealings in Smaller Firms', *Economic Journal* 104 (1994), pp. 37–53.

Hanley, K.W., 'The Underpricing of Initial Public Offerings and the Partial Adjustment Phenomenon', *Journal of Financial Economics* 37 (1993), pp. 231–250.

Hensler, D., Rutherford, R. and Springer, T., 'The Survival of Initial Public Offerings in the Aftermarket', *Journal of Financial Research* 20 (1997), pp. 93–110.

Hoque, H. and Lasfer, M., 'Directors' Dealing and Post-IPO Performance', *European Financial Management* 21 (2015), pp. 178–204.

Hughes, P.J. and Thakor, A.V., 'Litigation Risk, Intermediation and the Underpricing of Initial Public Offerings', *Review of Financial Studies* 5 (1992), pp. 709–742.

Ibbotson, R., 'Price Performance of Common Stock New Issues', *Journal of Financial Economics* 2 (1975), pp. 235–272.

Ibbotson, R., Sindelar, J. and Ritter, J., 'Initial Public Offerings', *Journal of Applied Corporate Finance* 1 (1988), pp. 37–45.

Jain, B.A. and Kini, O., 'The Post Issue Operating Performance of IPO firms', *Journal of Finance* 49 (1994), pp. 1699–1726.

Jain, B.A. and Kini, O., 'The Life Cycle of Initial Public Offerings', *Journal of Business Finance & Accounting* 26 (1999), pp. 1281–1307.

Jain, B.A. and Kini, O., 'Does the Presence of Venture Capitalists Improve the Survival Profile of IPO Firms?', *Journal of Business Finance & Accounting* 27 (2000), pp. 1139–1176.

Jain, B.A. and Martin, C., 'The Association Between Audit Quality and Post-IPO Performance: A Survival Analysis Approach', *Review of Accounting and Finance* 4 (2005), pp. 50–75.

Jenkinson, T.J and Ljungqvist, A.P., *Going Public: The Theory and Evidence on How Companies Raise Equity Finance* (Oxford University Press, 1996, 2001).

Jenkinson, T.J., 'Initial Public Offerings in the United Kingdom, the United States and Japan', *Journal of the Japanese and International Economies* 4 (1990), pp. 428–449.

Jensen, M. and Meckling, W., 'Theory of the Firm: Managerial Behaviour, Agency Costs and Ownership Structure', *Journal of Financial Economics* 3 (1976), pp. 306–360.

Keloharju, M., 'The Winner's Curse, Legal Liability and the Long-Run Performance of Initial Public Offerings in Finland', *Journal of Financial Economics* 34 (1993), pp. 251–277.

Khurshed, A. and Mudambi, R., 'The Short-Run Price Performance of Investment Trust IPOs on the UK Main Market', *Applied Financial Economics* 12 (2002), pp. 697–706.

Khurshed, A., 'The Google IPO: An Analysis', *Journal of Management Case Studies* (ICFAI) (2005), pp. 36–38.

Khurshed, A., Kostas, D., Mohamed, A. and Saadouni, B., 'Initial Public Offerings in the UK when-issued market,' *Journal of Corporate Finance* 49 (2018), pp. 1–14.

Kothari, S.P. and Warner, J.B., 'Measuring Long-Horizon Security Price Performance', *Journal of Financial Economics* 43 (1997), pp. 301–309.

Kunz, R.M. and Aggarwal, R., 'Why Initial Public Offerings are Underpriced: Evidence from Switzerland', *Journal of Banking and Finance* 18 (1994), pp. 705–724.

Lee, P.J., Taylor, S.L. and Walter, T.S., 'Australian IPO Pricing in the Short and Long-Run', University of Sydney Mimeograph (1994).

Levis, M., 'The Long-Run Performance of Initial Public Offerings: The UK Experience 1980–1988', *Financial Management* 22 (1993), pp. 28–41.

Liu, X. and Ritter, J.R., 'The Economic Consequences of IPO Spinning', *Review of Financial Studies* 23 (2010), pp. 2,024–2,059.

Ljungqvist, A.P., 'The Timing, Pricing and Long-Term Performance of Initial Public Offerings', Nuffield College, Oxford University Ph.D. thesis (1995).

Ljungqvist, A.P., 'When do Firms Go Public? Poisson Evidence from Germany', University of Oxford working paper (1995).

Ljungqvist, A.P., 'IPO Long-Run Performance: Fact or Fiction?', Oxford University School of Management Studies Mimeograph (1996).

Ljungqvist, A.P. and Wilhelm, W.J., 'IPO Pricing in the Dot-com Bubble', *Journal of Finance* 58 (2003), pp. 723–752.

Ljungqvist, A.P., Jenkinson, T. J. and Wilhelm, W.J., 'Global Integration of Primary Equity Markets: The Role of US Banks and US Investors', *Review of Financial Studies* 16 (2003), pp. 63–99.

Ljungqvist, A., Nanda, V. and Singh, R., 'Hot Markets, Investor Sentiment, and IPO Pricing', *Journal of Business* 79 (2006), pp. 1667–1702.

Mikkelson, W.H., Partch, M.M. and Shah, K., 'Ownership and Operating Performance of Companies that Go Public', *Journal of Financial Economics* 44 (1997), pp. 281–307.

Miller, E.M., 'Risk, Uncertainty and Divergence of Opinion', *Journal of Finance* 32 (1977), pp. 1151–1168.

Muscarella, C. and Vetsuypens, M., 'A Simple Test of Baron's Model of IPO Under-pricing', *Journal of Financial Economics* 24 (1989), pp. 125–135.

Purnanandam, A. and Swaminathan, B., 'Are IPOs Really Underpriced?', *Review of Financial Studies* 17 (2004), pp. 811–848.

Rajan, R. and Servaes, H., 'Analyst Following of Initial Public Offerings', *Journal of Finance* 52 (1997), pp. 507–529.

Reilly, F.K., 'New Issues Revisited', *Financial Management* (Winter 1977), pp. 28–42.

Ritter, J.R., 'The Long-Run Performance of Initial Public Offerings', *Journal of Finance* 46 (1991), pp. 3–27.

Rock, K., 'Why New Issues are Underpriced', *Journal of Financial Economics* 15 (1986), pp. 187–212.

Rudd, J.S., 'Underwriter Price Support and the IPO Underpricing Puzzle', *Journal of Financial Economics* 34 (1993), pp. 135–151.

Sefcik, E. S. and Thompson, R., 'An Approach to Statistical Inference in Cross-Sectional Models with Security Abnormal Returns as Dependent Variable', *Journal of Accounting Research* 24:2 (1986).

Shleifer, A. and Vishny, R., 'Large Stakeholders and Corporate Control', *Journal of Political Economy* 94 (1986), pp. 461–488.

Stoughton, N.M. and Zechner, J., 'IPO Mechanisms, Monitoring and Ownership Structure', *Journal of Financial Economics* 49 (1998), pp. 45–77.

Tinic, S., 'Anatomy of the IPOs of Common Stock', *Journal of Finance* 43 (1988), pp. 789–822.

Vos, E.A. and Cheung, J., 'New Zealand IPO Underpricing: The Reputation Factor', *Small Enterprise Research* 1 (1992), pp. 13–22.

Weiss, H.K., 'The Underpricing of Initial Public Offerings and Partial Adjustment Phenomenon', *Journal of Financial Economics* 34 (1993), pp. 231–250.

Welch, I., 'Seasoned Offerings, Imitation Costs and the Underpricing of IPOs', *Journal of Finance* 44 (1989), pp. 421–449.

Welch, I., 'Equity Offerings Following the IPO: Theory and Evidence', *Journal of Corporate Finance* 2 (1996), pp. 227–259.

Index

Note: Page numbers in *italic* refer to Figures; those in **bold** refer to Tables

143

Lightning Source UK Ltd.
Milton Keynes UK
UKHW021033091019
351281UK00003B/69/P